Sins of the Fathers

*How national repentance
removes obstacles for revival*

Brian Mills
and
Roger Mitchell

Sovereign World

Sovereign World Ltd
PO Box 777
Tonbridge
Kent
TN11 0ZS
England

ISBN: 1 85240 253 9

This Sovereign World book is distributed in North America by Renew Books, a ministry of Gospel Light, Ventura, California, USA. For a free catalog of resources from Renew Books/Gospel Light, please contact your Christian supplier or call 1–800–4–GOSPEL.

Typeset by CRB Associates, Reepham, Norfolk
Printed in the UK by Clays Ltd, St Ives plc

Contents

Acknowledgements

We wish to record our deep appreciation to the following for their significant help in enabling us to write this book:

Sandy Waldron, who has fused our two styles into one and edited the book; Lynn Green for his willingness to let us include some of his original material on the Crusades in chapter 4; our long-time friend John Pressdee, who has led Prayer and Reconciliation expeditions to many nations in Europe and the Middle East, for chapter 10; Chris Seaton who assisted with material on Africa; Harry Sprange and Kath Fathers who helped us with some of the historical material for chapter 14; Kate Young for making available correspondence on opposition to the opium trade discussed in chapter 12; David Sladden who has contributed research on issues where our knowledge was very limited.

The many people whom we have met along the way who, often without knowing it, have contributed something more to our understanding of our corporate guilt; others who just 'happen' to have sent us material that we needed at the right time.

We have been conscious that, despite the length of time it has taken us to complete this book, God has had his finger on so much of what we have written. Thank you, Father.

Roger Mitchell and Brian Mills
Summer 1999

Foreword

The importance of this book for Britain and the world can hardly be overstated. I have prayed for its writing for years. I believe in its message and practise it. I will spend the rest of my life pleading that people read these pages and apply these truths, not just British people, for this is a message that can be applied to all nations.

This book contains a radical thesis but Roger Mitchell and Brian Mills are not theoreticians or theological sophisticates titillating us with new ideas, they are pioneers who have recklessly applied the cross to their own pride. They have personally humbled themselves to the dust over Britain's sins in front of real people in real places. Great healing has been the result.

As the son of parents who were taught to sing 'Rule Britannia' in school, yet raised me surrounded by brown Maori faces in the Islands at the ends of the earth, I read these pages with tears. Through this book I could glimpse the beginning of a new day for my nation and the many other nations influenced by British authority. Today's British intercessors could be the catalyst for a season of cleansing and healing for our cultural and spiritual foundations. A kind of jubilee could come as the shame of Britain is turned to glory through the mystery of the cross.

This is a breakthrough book for international intercessors; part of a growing body of resources exploring the subject of priestly mediation and identificational repentance. This is the best book yet. The authors masterfully tackle problems that have perplexed Christians for generations. Here we learn how to remove the hindrances to sustained revival and national renewal along with the key to a rekindling of Britain's zeal for missions.

You will have to discover the remarkable content of this book for yourself, however I long for you to know Roger and Brian as people because the actions of a true reconciler always speak louder than their words.

They are veteran Christian leaders with a worldwide vision who embody the best of what we foreigners admire in the English personality. In humility mingled with strength of resolve, they both radiate the beauty of Jesus. These are men of dignity, love and humour who live to honour the good in others.

We of other nations sometimes reflexively associate England with arrogance but in Roger and Brian we see another truth about their nation. Because of their humility and that of others like them, I have come to love and admire the redemptive gifts of English people and to expect dramatic reports of justice and reconciliation from the British Isles. We need their leadership.

Most impressive to me was the seven-week Prayer Journey recently completed in Australia. A British team, led by the authors and commissioned by several movements in London, traversed Australia expressing deep repentance toward those still dealing with residual pain stemming from the treatment of Aboriginals and convicts under British authority.

Immediately following this historic initiative, I had the privilege of sitting with Aboriginal leaders in the Australian Parliament as they processed what had just happened. Their comments left me in no doubt that the principles demonstrated in this book are nation changing. If you want to change your world, read on.

John Dawson, Founder
International Reconciliation Coalition
Auckland, New Zealand, 1999

Introduction

'We can't ignore the sins of the Fathers' proclaimed the headline of a review of two books published at the same time, highlighting the sins of Catholic priests. The world is interested in the sins of the Church. Those who fall from grace risk a damaging exposé of their private lives.

But sin is not only personal, it is also corporate. It is not only current, it is also historic. It is not only of the Church, it is also of every nation and every institution.

The 'sins of the fathers' is what this book is about – the sins of our forefathers, to be more precise. Sin, whenever and however it is committed, is, first and foremost, a violation of God's law. But it inevitably is also a violation of the rights of others. Sin is never private – others are always implicated, hurt or offended. In order for the slate to be wiped clean, sin needs to be punished, or atoned for, and forgiven.

Of course, for the individual, what Christ did on the cross is fully effective in providing an answer to our guilt and a means of forgiveness. But for each person that atonement has to be appropriated to be applicable. Sin has to be confessed and turned from in order for its eternal effects to be dealt with.

But what about corporate sin? Who takes responsibility for it and how? Is it important? Does Christ's sacrifice deal with the accumulated aggregate of the sin of many individuals acting together?

We want to look at some of these questions – not to wallow in gloom and doom over our corporate sin but to face the reality of sin's effects in the lives of countless people around the world. We want to explore what the sins of this nation have caused in terms of misery, hate, fear and repetitive evil. We want to do this because we believe that God is longing to deal with our past.

At the same time we rejoice over the way that the United Kingdom has been a blessing in the past to many other nations. Some of our inventions (like the printing press) have been exported. Our education system and parliamentary democracy have been the envy of the world and have been replicated elsewhere. Freedom of speech (so much appreciated here) has often been sought after in those places where repression and restriction have prevailed instead. Nations throughout the world are profoundly grateful too for the missionary thrust of previous generations over many centuries from these shores.

Many prayers have been uttered and many prophecies have been given about this nation – the United Kingdom – becoming a blessing to the world. Many long for this to happen, but do our motives need questioning? Are we perhaps seeking some glory in it for ourselves? Or are we genuinely thinking of the good of those nations?

If that blessing is ever to be poured out, do we not have to face and remove the blocks to the gospel which at present exist and hinder such blessing? We cannot ignore what the leaders of this 'Christian' nation have sanctioned in the past. We believe that their decisions and subsequent actions have impaired and impeded the spread of the gospel.

We have been a pioneer nation. We have also been a missionary nation. We have explored the world, established our colonies, signed our treaties, and built our Empire. But as we have done all this, we have frequently carried a hidden agenda that has been basically selfish. In pursuing national interests, we have been politically motivated, power grabbing, resource stripping, and murderous. Consequently, the message carried by Christian missionaries has at times been defiled.

We write this book with a positive end in view. We want to see this nation change, other nations change, and God's love flow out to previously disenfranchised groups of people. But our history often stands in the way. We want to write from our heart as well as from our head. From our personal perspective as well as from what we believe to be God's perspective.

We write not only to provoke discussion, but also to convey what we believe is a most vital message for a new millennium. We pray for public confession, statements of apology, and acts of reconciliation wherever and whenever appropriate – by Church and national leaders.

Before we start, we apologise for any offence that may be unwittingly caused – particularly to those whose personal history may possibly be entwined with our national history.

Chapter 1

The Start of a Journey

We were about 30,000 feet up, halfway across Russia, en route to Korea. The two of us were travelling to the Gideon's Army gathering of the Spiritual Warfare Network, which Peter Wagner had formed as part of the Prayer Track of the AD 2000 Movement. We were talking together in the corridor of the plane, sharing insights that we had gained about the spiritual forces at work in our own country. Julie Anderson, leader of Prayer for the Nation, was in the group, and Bob Dunnett, leader of Prayer for Revival, was elsewhere on the plane.

The conversation turned to the Prayer for the Poor Conferences which Roger had hosted at Ashburnham in 1989 and 1991. At both conferences delegates had been led to identify a spirit of death that seemed to be at work in the history of relationships between the Church, the State and the poor – in fact, a number of those involved had also encountered the self-same spirit in intensely personal experiences of near death by accident or sudden sickness.

The phrase 'spirit of death' triggered a reaction in my spirit too. Over the years I had discovered that God gives burdens in prayer. When He does, you know they are from Him. For me those burdens had been accompanied by inexplicable weeping, and had been followed by divine appointments, a desire for further knowledge about the subject, and a longing to pray with any who had the same burden.

As we stood in the corridor sharing together, we started to weep and to pray and prophesy. We thought we were prophesying into each other's lives, but it later emerged that the essence of what we shared was what God intended to do in the days to come in Korea. God was there. Others watched on with some embarrassment. Suddenly a tannoy announcement came through asking for a doctor – somebody had been taken ill. We prayed against a 'spirit of death' operating on that plane.

I had started out on this journey towards an understanding of 'identificational repentance' when, in 1985, Suzette Hattingh visited England for the first time. I had been invited to the home of Alan and Eileen Vincent (two church leaders now resident in the USA) to meet her. Suzette, who used to lead intercession for Reinhard Bonnke's missions, teaches on the subject of prayer and is a powerful woman of prayer! As we chatted, she started to share her belief that a 'spirit of murder' was over this nation. The more we talked, the more we realised she could be right. Our ancient monuments were nearly all in memory of our achievements in war – places where blood had been shed. Our number one historic tourist attraction was the Tower of London, renowned as a place of torture and beheadings of royalty, rebels and foreigners. It seemed that we prided ourselves on our blood-shedding past and victories in battle. Not only that, over 4.7 million foetuses have been aborted over a thirty-year period.[1] And we have one of the highest suicide rates in Western Europe.

As we prayed about this, the six of us in the room began to weep, not quietly, but with deep sobs. I was beside myself with anguish. For what must have been an hour we wept together. It was the first time that such weeping in prayer had gripped me. Since that time whenever anyone in conversation has referred to murder or death or bloodshed in relation to our nation, the same reaction has occurred. God, it seemed, had implanted something deep within me, but I did not know what to do about it. I carried this knowledge, or burden, with me for eight years. The finger of God seemed to be pointed at our murderous past.

Once in Korea, we were both involved in different ways in the conference. Our time there was to prove life-changing. We were staying on the Methodist Church's Kwang Lim prayer mountain, one of 500 owned by Korean churches. It is a beautiful facility, with residential accommodation for about 400 people, and a modern church building that could probably seat 1,000 Koreans, though probably a few less Western Europeans! It also has one hundred prayer cubicles leading onto a beautiful mountain walk, laid out with life-size replicas from the scenes of Christ's life. It is all conducive to prayer. As well as the 300 delegates from around the world, staying on the mountain was a team of about thirty inter-cessors who had come just to pray.

The conference timetable was full. Sessions had been planned with the intention of giving delegates from every region of the world a chance to share what had been happen-ing in spiritual warfare. But God did something special that took the whole conference in a different direction.

Before giving his report, Paul Ariga, a Japanese leader, in a totally uncultural response, knelt and wept in front of his fellow Asian delegates, asking for forgiveness for the atro-cities that his country had committed in the Second World War. Most of us were glad this was happening – it needed to, we thought. Japan had invaded China, Taiwan, Korea, the Philippines and Burma. Terrible atrocities had been inflicted upon the local populations. America had suffered the agony of the invasion of Pearl Harbour. Britain, Australia and the Pacific Islands had also been affected, although for the most part these countries were not themselves invaded.

The next day, however, something happened I was not quite so ready for. During their session, white North Amer-icans started to confess the atrocities their forefathers had committed against the native North American Indians in the pioneer period. This was different. Japan I could understand, but these events had taken place well over two hundred years ago. What difference could this acknowledgement make to history? You can't change history, I thought. Yet, my mind ran, the fruits of history are seen in the present day, and if the fruits of those historical atrocities were being expressed today in resistance to the 'white man's gospel', then something had to be done about them.

Suddenly I had one of those revelations that God some-times gives. The sins that these mature Christian leaders were confessing were actually sins that had been transferred from my own country at the time when the Pilgrim Fathers settled America. The Pilgrim Fathers were missionaries – not just religious refugees, as some suppose. Dutch and German Christians came too. They all had a common understanding: they were Protestant Reformers. In their wake had followed others with different motives.

Unfortunately there was a bloody side to the early history of Puritanism. Following the Acts of Supremacy and Uniformity in 1560 under Elizabeth I, attempts were made to impose the Reformation on Ireland. Later Oliver Cromwell, believing he had a biblical mandate, used military might to enforce Protestantism on the Irish, although political motives were also involved. Thus, from the mid-sixteenth century onwards, the taking of land and the imposition of the Christian faith by force was accepted practice. At the same time, America was being settled by Christians with pure motives, desirous of establishing something for and of God in the New World. Unwittingly these emigrants took with them the seeds of division and of conflict that were plaguing Christendom back home. A 'spirit of murder' was unintentionally exported with them, along with the same cultural and religious attitudes that had characterised their lifestyle at home.

Roger and I began to share our thoughts with one another, only to realise we were on the same track. What should we do about it? In how many other nations had something similar happened? We agreed that this was not the time to act, but perhaps an opportunity might arise later. We decided to sleep on it. The finger of God was pointing at us.

The next day was to be extraordinary. At the early morning prayer meeting for Northern Europeans, the two of us shared what had been happening and asked for prayer for wisdom and understanding – and for an opportunity to share what God had begun to lay upon us. As we prayed, we started to weep. The horror of our nation's sin and the anguish we felt as British citizens began to hit us. We felt shame, guilt and remorse, as if we ourselves had been personally responsible. 'Lord, help us,' we cried. 'Our sin is so great, we are overwhelmed.'

Neither was it just restricted to America. We began to realise that Australia, Malaysia, India, Ireland, Africa, the West Indies – in fact everywhere that the British Empire had spread – were also affected by a similar spirit. We had been guilty of pillage, plundering the wealth of nations; we had raped womenfolk; we had shed the blood of innocents; we had taken land by force or by trickery; we had made slaves of others, treating them as less than human. And although we had taken the gospel to many of these nations at the same time, the message was defiled because of what accompanied it.

Later, as we went to breakfast, a Malaysian lady came up to me and told me that in her regional prayer meeting that morning she and her fellow delegates had been asking God for forgiveness for their bad attitudes towards the British because of what the British had done to their nation. 'What things?' I asked, and she told me! It was hard to take breakfast through tears!

Later in the day, we had an opportunity to ask publicly for forgiveness for the sins of England (we didn't feel we could speak on behalf of Scotland, Ireland and Wales at that time) in its history. We named some of the sins, some of the countries affected, but acknowledged that we needed help. The task was so big, our sin stretched around the world, and it had impeded the gospel. We asked for prayer and humbled ourselves. An African brother prayed for us along with the lady from Malaysia and they prayed with tremendous passion and understanding, as well as with tears. We ourselves were broken in spirit.

The floodgates had begun to be opened. During the rest of that conference people from nation after nation came to us and mentioned one issue after another they were aware of that implicated Britain and needed to be dealt with. Since then we both have had some extraordinary 'divine appointments' when God has brought us into contact with Christian leaders from around the world who have acquainted us, without our prompting, with the sins of our nation towards theirs.

We began to feel in our emotions and spirits what we already knew in our minds, that around the world we as a nation are perceived as arrogant and proud. The English think they know best and present a patronising attitude. We cannot be trusted to keep our promises. We renege on our treaties. We always act in the best interests of ourselves, whatever the implications for other nations. In personal terms we name such behaviour selfishness. It is no less selfish when it is viewed in corporate or national terms. In the Scriptures such attitudes are condemned as sin. *'God resists the proud, but gives grace to the humble'* (Proverbs 3:34 NIV; see also James 4:6, 1 Peter 5:5). His finger is pointed at us.

Of course pride and arrogance are not the sole possessions of the English. In an age of nationalism and ethnic identity we see pride emerge in many forms. Sometimes pride is good and positive – pride in achievement, pride in appearance, pride in quality. A nation can be justly proud of its valuable contributions to the well-being of humankind.

Pride is not justified, however, when others are demeaned or denigrated, denied basic human rights or defiled in order to reinforce the superiority of one race, class or creed over another. Each nation or group is responsible for its own pride. None of us can excuse ourselves by pointing the finger at others. Nor can we hide behind another's more guilty past as a way of countenancing our own. We can neither excuse nor ignore our own guilt.

If God resists the proud, then we had better humble ourselves and so get rid of our pride. That pride is detestable and unjustified. If we are going to pave the way for blessing to flow to the nations, then we have to come in the opposite spirit – a spirit of humility and repentance.

In Luke 11 Jesus gives us an interesting sequel to His famous words on prayer. He says,

> *'Any kingdom divided against itself is laid waste; and a house divided against itself falls. And if Satan also is divided against himself, how shall his kingdom stand?'*
>
> (Luke 11:17–18)

He then goes on to challenge the opinion of religious leaders that He was casting out devils by Beelzebub, the prince of demons, by saying,

> *'... if I cast out demons by the finger of God, then the kingdom of God has come upon you.'*   (Luke 11:20)

We believe God's finger is pointed at our nation in accusation, just as it was when, in the time of Daniel, the invisible hand at Belteshazzar's feast wrote the words *'Mene, mene, tekel upharsin'* on the wall. The meaning of the word *upharsin* is 'Your kingdom has been divided and given over to the Medes and Persians' (Daniel 5:26–8).

In many respects our 'British' kingdom is divided. The British Empire is no more and the 'United Kingdom' is not really united except politically. And even that is open to change! It is made up of four nations, each with its own identity and political parties campaigning for autonomous political power. But we are also divided in other ways: economically and spiritually.

In Daniel the finger of God is pointed in judgement. But, as is evident from the verse just quoted from Luke 11, Jesus is more concerned for the kingdom of God to come through His driving out of demons by the finger of God. So are we. Whilst the finger of God may be pointed at us in judgement chapter by chapter, our heart's desire is for Jesus Christ our Lord to start driving out the demons that have fed so much on the legacy of our past unconfessed, unacknowledged and unforgiven sin.

Some aspects of our history are good. We have exported education, medicine, government, creativity, and the gospel! For example, we have brought infrastructures of roads and rail links. We have taught skills which have helped many nations to develop their own natural resources. The civilisation brought by our pioneers has changed many an underdeveloped society. We have taken new ideas for living; we have built hospitals and sought to eradicate many traditional diseases; we have started schools and sought to teach illiterate peoples how to read and write; we introduced new systems of government (not always with immediate approval). And above all, many of our pioneers brought with them the gospel which helped to shape the lives and values of the people. That gospel, first brought with sacrifice and tears, has today resulted in a burgeoning church-growth movement in many of our former colonies.

However, the good never outweighs or cancels the bad. It is the bad which concerns us. It can neither be excused nor condoned. It has to be faced and repented of, particularly where a legacy of hate, fear, suspicion and antagonism against the British, especially the English, persists, and where resistance to the Christian gospel has been the result.

We desire with all our hearts for the kingdom of God to come with compassion and with power, penetrating every level of society, and spreading into every nation of the world where we have, or had, historical relationships.

In writing this book we are constantly facing challenges that we cannot meet. Each chapter should be a book in itself. We are not writing from an historical point of view but we are informed and challenged by our history, and ashamed by some of it. No comment on history is conclusive, nor exhaustive. Inevitably we are selective. We are trying to be factual, but recognise that we cannot give the whole story. We are not historians, but are seeking to learn from our history.

Note

1.   Figures provided by Care Trust.

Chapter 2

Britain's Past – Can We Face It?

In the nations of the West we have been very individualistic in our thinking. It is hard for us to understand that God treats people corporately and that judgement comes on a nation when it turns away from God's purposes.

I first began to think about this issue after being struck by Jesus' last words to his disciples as recorded by Luke:

> 'He said to them, "Thus it is written, that the Christ should suffer and rise again from the dead the third day; and that repentance for forgiveness of sins should be proclaimed in His name to all the nations, beginning from Jerusalem."'
>
> (Luke 24:46–7)

I began to ask myself whether there was any significance in the fact that Jesus had said that the gospel would be preached to all *nations*. Could He really mean nations should repent, I wondered, rather than individuals within those nations?

My thinking led me to verses in Hosea which refer specifically to the fact that the Messiah would rise on the third day. Although Jesus of course spoke of this dying and rising many times, as far as I am aware this is the only Old Testament Scripture which specifically refers to dying and rising again on the third day, and must have been the verse Jesus was interpreting when He made His claims.

> 'Come, let us return to the Lord.
> For He has torn us but He will heal us;
> He has wounded us, but He will bandage us.
> He will revive us after two days;
> He will raise us up on the third day

That we may live before Him.
So let us know, let us press on to know the Lord.
His going forth is as certain as the dawn;
And He will come to us like the rain;
Like the spring rain watering the earth.'   (Hosea 6:1–3)

Hosea is referring here to a dying and a rising that will bring about the dawn of the purposes of God and the coming of the Spirit. Jesus fulfilled in a personal way what was prophesied as a corporate dying and rising. The Scripture says: *'He will revive us ... He will raise us up.'* But who are those who are torn and dead? This reference can be to none other than the corporate nationhood of Israel, and the nation is dead because *'... they employ violence, so that bloodshed follows bloodshed. Therefore the land mourns. And everyone who lives in it languishes...'* (Hosea 4:2f). There is a death that comes upon a nation if that nation is guilty of sin and behaviour corporately that brings bloodshed both upon its own people and upon the peoples of other lands. Right in the roots of the Old Testament we see not only the individual atonement for individual sin that is clearly foreshadowed in the temple sacrifices but also here the corporate sin that brings judgement on a people and needs to be dealt with.

Let us look at the example of Jeremiah. Now Jeremiah walked with God. I find no evidence that Jeremiah was anything other than a true prophet of God, yet he had to be carried off into captivity along with his fellow countrymen and women. Judgement had been building up against his nation for many generations, and he happened to be alive at the time when it came to fulfilment. His ministry and righteousness were not sufficient to turn the nation into a place that would receive the fullness of God's will.

If we are going to get to grips with national sin we have got to understand that corporate sin does exist. By **individual** sin I mean sin committed by an individual for which he or she is responsible before God. By **corporate** sin I mean the sin committed by a group of people of which an individual is a part. The individual may not actually have committed the sin personally and may not even have been alive when the sin was actually perpetrated, but he or she has a solidarity, a relationship, with the people whom God holds responsible for the sin, or at the very least is implicated in its results.

Jesus recognised whole people groups as under the judgement of God. He pulls no punches as He denounces whole sectors of society:

> *'Woe to you, scribes and Pharisees . . .'* (see Matthew 23:15)

> *' . . . woe to you who are rich now . . . '* (Luke 6:24)

> *'Woe to you, lawyers . . . '* (Luke 11:46)

> *' . . . Woe to you, Chorazim! Woe to you, Bethsaida! . . . But it will be more tolerable for Tyre and Sidon in the judgement than for you . . . '* (Luke 10:13–14)

Does that mean that if you happened to be a Pharisee there was no hope for you? There was hope for the Pharisee who had enough courage to go and see Jesus by night. There was hope too for his friend Joseph of Arimathea as, along with Nicodemus, he moved from being a secret disciple to a public one as they boldly went to ask for the body of Jesus after His crucifixion. Personally they had got hold of the grace of God and had found freedom, but it was a hard thing for them to do because their whole social group was under the judgement of God. It was a hard thing for a Pharisee to comprehend the gospel of Christ and it was a hard thing for a rich man to enter the kingdom of heaven – as hard as a virgin birth! With human beings it is impossible but with God all things are possible (Matthew 19:26).

There is corporate sin and there is corporate judgement. Jesus lamented over the city of Jerusalem:

> *'O Jerusalem, Jerusalem . . . How often I wanted to gather your children together, just as a hen gathers her brood under her wings, and you would not have it.'* (Luke 13:34)

Jerusalem missed the day of her visitation by the Lord Jesus Christ, and yet Jesus commanded His disciples, *'Stay in Jerusalem until you receive power from on high.'* Wasn't that a visitation? It was indeed, but only one hundred and twenty people had the privilege of sharing in it. Thank God, another 3120 were saved as a result of it and indeed later, by the grace of God, all Jerusalem was full of his teaching (Acts 5:28). However, there were thousands of people living in Jerusalem at the time and the fact remains that the city was corporately under the judgement of God and in AD 70 it was destroyed.

Of course, this principle is demonstrated again and again in the Old Testament with the prophets' cries of *'Woe to you, Ammon ... Moab ... Edom...'* and so on, with the Word of the Lord coming to whole nations. When Jonah eventually went to Nineveh he did not preach just to the king – he went to the whole city and proclaimed, *'Yet forty days and Nineveh will be overthrown'* (Jonah 3:4). The whole city responded – even down to the cattle and the sheep – and was saved.

This also explains God's dealings with the Canaanite peoples. The judgement of God was over these nations because they had reached such a level of immorality and occult through their materialism over many generations, that if they had been allowed to continue to exist before Christ came with the means to provide forgiveness and reconciliation, God's purposes on the earth would have been totally destroyed. If this were not true, then how could the God of love, who is like our Lord Jesus, possibly destroy them? It was because corporate sin had reached such a level it had to be dealt with. Yet His heart was still towards those nations, and that is why there was still the possibility for the harlot, Rahab, to be saved by placing the red cord in her window, reaching down one thousand years or more to the blood of Jesus shed on the cross, with the result that she and her household were saved.

In Revelation chapters 2 and 3, the Word of the Lord is addressed to whole churches and this is further evidence in itself of the existence of corporate solidarities. Each church is a company of believers and is clearly identified as having an angel. This angelic spiritual presence comes by the blood of Jesus and the Holy Spirit (Revelation 1:4–5) to somehow form, guard and protect them, and to be a minister to develop that church. In five of the seven messages to the churches the whole church is commanded to repent, and at Ephesus the people of God are warned that if they do not, Jesus will remove their lampstand from them and with it the light or star which represents the angel. Jesus clearly regards these churches as having a corporate identity which makes them responsible before God for what they do – a corporate identity held together by angelic ministry.

Jesus goes even further than this and suggests that not only are corporate sin and corporate judgement a reality, but also that it is possible for whole sectors of society to be demonised – that is held together by demonic activity. Jesus tells a parable of a house that has been swept clean. In Luke's version of the story it is simply a cautionary tale about the deliverance of a demonised man, with the message that if the house is not properly cleansed (i.e. if the person does not repent, receive forgiveness, and then be filled with the Spirit of God), seven spirits which are worse than the first will come back and inhabit it. In Matthew's version, however, the story concludes with the words: *'That is the way it will also be with this evil generation'* (Matthew 12:45). If you warn a person about persistent sin but he chooses to go on doing it, he gives place to the enemy and eventually, as in the case of Judas Iscariot, the enemy comes and takes him over altogether. Jesus indicates that a similar process can occur in a whole generation of people. If a whole generation constantly sins in a particular way – for example in a wrong attitude or action towards individuals or groups or other nations – they will make room for the enemy and eventually they will begin to be inhabited by satanic powers.

At many different moments in history over the last two thousand years, as far as the United Kingdom is concerned, there has been a move of the Spirit which has impacted a whole generation. But instead of this move serving the purposes of God, it has again and again been used to protect and serve the interest of one group against another, or this nation against other nations, so that the religion, as it has then become, is solely the means of legitimating one group's power against another's. When this happens, Jesus tells us, the last state of that generation will be worse than the first. This is the reason why it has been so hard for the nation to experience and sustain revival.

The Scriptures point to the fact that there are levels of involvement in corporate sin. The first level to identify is **associated guilt**: we are implicated because of the actions of our fathers. Our generation is implicated in acts carried out under the name of the United Kingdom all over the world, some of which we will look at in detail in this book. To take just one example, in 1875 the British Government made a treaty with the Sultans in Malaysia, making it unlawful to evangelise any Muslims and allowing the Muslims to remain in power just as long as they co-operated with the British Government (see chapter 9). This was a terrible contract for Church and State to agree to. Although we were not alive when this treaty was made, as British people we have a part to play in identificational repentance over this issue. This is **associated guilt**. We did not actually commit the sin personally but we are a part of the nation that did.

The writers of the Old Testament certainly understood associated guilt. Nehemiah, Isaiah, Daniel, and others all confessed it:

> *'O Lord God of heaven ... let Thine ear now be attentive and Thine eyes open to hear the prayer of Thy servant which I am praying before Thee now, day and night, on behalf of the sons of Israel Thy servants, confessing the sins of the sons of Israel which we have sinned against Thee; I and my father's house have sinned.'*   (Nehemiah 1:6)

> *'Then I said, "Woe is me for I am ruined! Because I am a man of unclean lips, And I live among a people of unclean lips ... "'*   (Isaiah 6:5)

> *'Open shame belongs to us, O Lord, to our kings, our princes, and our fathers, because we have sinned against Thee.'*
>   (Daniel 9:8)

In each case it is not so much that Nehemiah or Daniel or Isaiah had personally participated in the sin concerned but because their nation had sinned, they were associated with it.

The second level of guilt is **actual guilt**. For example, if there is immorality in the Church, it has to be dealt with – the Bible says so. Paul gives an example of this in 1 Corinthians 5:

> *'It is actually reported that there is immorality among you, and immorality of such a kind as does not exist even*

among the Gentiles, that someone has his father's wife ...
Your boasting is not good. Do you not know that a little
leaven leavens the whole lump of dough? Clean out the old
leaven, that you may be a new lump, just as you are in fact
unleavened. For Christ our Passover also has been sacrificed.'
(1 Corinthians 5:6–7)

Or perhaps there is partiality in the Church and if it is not
eliminated there will be actual contemporary guilt affecting
the whole body. James makes this clear:

'My brethren, do not hold your faith in our glorious Lord Jesus
Christ with an attitude of personal favouritism. For if a man
comes into your assembly with a gold ring and dressed in fine
clothes, and there also comes in a poor man in dirty clothes,
and you pay special attention to the one who is wearing the
fine clothes, and say, "You sit here in a good place," and you
say to the poor man, "You stand over there, or sit down by my
footstool," have you not made distinctions among yourselves,
and become judges with evil motives?'   (James 2:1–4)

If we do not take action to eradicate sin in the Church, we
become implicated in it.

The third level is **vicarious guilt**. In Isaiah 53 we find the
picture of the Suffering Servant who bore our sins: our sins
were laid on Him; He carried all our sicknesses and our griefs.
It is the heart of God to invade the place of sickness, pain,
sin, or demonic oppression and to carry it all away in His
own body. That is what Jesus did. Only He could do this
pioneering work for He did not sin personally. But we are
sinners, and we carry associated guilt or are actually guilty.
Jesus identified with all the sins of humankind and that was
how the love of God, the passion of Jesus, invaded the
greatest problem of all, that men and women are alienated
from God. Ephesians chapter 2 leaves us in no doubt that
such reconciliation is possible and that the cross has
achieved it. Writing of the reconciling of Jews and Gentiles
Paul says:

'But now in Christ Jesus, you who formerly were far off have
been brought near by the blood of Christ. For he himself is our

> *peace who made both groups into one and broke down the*
> *barrier of the dividing wall.'*   (Ephesians 2:13–14)

As Jesus atoned and carried vicariously my sin for me, surely once this has taken place I will, with others in the Body, want to play my part in carrying the guilt of corporate human sin. Atone for it I cannot, but repent of it I can! Can there be any greater way that *'the manifold wisdom of God might now be made known through the church to the rulers and authorities in the heavenly places'* (Ephesians 3:10)? We call this **identificational repentance**. Some prefer to call it identificational confession because they point out that Jesus didn't repent for the sins of the world, so why should we? However, our understanding is that Jesus did **more** than repent! He **atoned**. He **became** the sins of the world.

> *'He made Him who knew no sin to be sin on our behalf, that*
> *we might become the righteousness of God in Him.'*
>   (2 Corinthians 5:21)

This is what we can't do, because we are sinners. Jesus made vicarious atonement for us. What we **can** do is take the lesser position of vicarious repentance. If people wish to use the word confession instead of repentance, we are content just so long as this is not a proud unwillingness on their part to identify with the sins of others, such as their fathers' or their nation's. This would be to make themselves better than Jesus who was prepared even to **become** the sins of the fathers and nations of the world.

Our identificational repentance will not automatically bring salvation to everyone in a nation or city. But it will lead to increased conversions and open up the way for revival. The Old Testament clearly documents the process whereby identificational repentance brings about massive change in the history of a city and nation. Both Nehemiah's and Daniel's repentance in Nehemiah 1:4–11 and Daniel 9:3–19 respectively are shown in causal relationship to the ending of the captivity and the return of the Jews to restore Jerusalem. Nehemiah's prayer was followed by King Artaxerxes sending him back to Jerusalem to rebuild it and Daniel's by a visitation from Gabriel who decreed the beginning of the end of the captivity. In New Testament terms the corporate effect of the atonement on the sins and judgement on the nation secured at least four results:

- the visitation of Pentecost,
- the establishing of the Church,
- the filling of Jerusalem with Jesus' teaching, and
- the continuation through the gospel of the Abrahamic covenant that all the families of the earth would be blessed.

Perhaps the most notable contemporary example of the impact of identificational repentance is the case of the Argentinian city of Resistencia documented by Ed Silvoso in his book *That None Should Perish*.[1] Here the repentance by the pastors in unity together for the divisions of the past led, among other things, to a 300 per cent growth in the Church. In contemporary Britain we are already witnessing a new level of responsiveness to the gospel seen in the prisons and among the gypsies and recently in the unprecedented take-up of the Alpha courses. We believe that in the years ahead, as we respond to what God is saying to us, we will see further evidences of revival in the Church which will in themselves be proof of our thesis. By that time we hope to be in a better position to make known some of the specific contemporary issues involving identificational repentance which until then it would be contentious or even libellous to document.

The act of identifying the sins of a nation and confessing them will lead to the revoking of God's judgement over that land so that there will be an increase in people turning back to God. A degree of judgement has been lifted off the nation in question, and so it will be easier for individuals to respond to God's voice and repent in their own right for their personal sin, and easier for leaders in society to bring about change. But our responding to God in repentance does not actually save people. Individuals have to respond to the gospel for themselves. What we are doing is dealing with the darkness which is preventing individual people from seeing the light and preventing the leaders of a nation from leading it in the way that it should go.

The Scriptures reveal that there are justice norms for nations. The Bible makes it clear that there are certain standards of behaviour that God expects of the nations irrespective of whether they are His special people – the Jews – or other neighbouring nations. God will hold them responsible for their behaviour whether or not it impinges upon His people. It is clear that the main purpose of the Jewish nation was to be a blessing to all other tribes and nations. That was God's word to Abraham and when the Jews lost this inheritance, Jesus said it was because they had failed to be a house of prayer for all nations (Matthew 21:12–13).

God has all the nations on His heart and He deals with each nation according to the light its people have received. However, the Scriptures make it plain that there is a certain amount of light which He expects all of the nations to walk by. This is very evident in the first chapters of Amos. In addition to the North and South of Israel, God denounces six nations (grouped in pairs) and in each instance, the Scriptures say:

> *'For three transgressions and for four I will not revoke its punishment'.*   (Amos 1:3, 6, 9, 11, 13; and 2:1, 4, 6)

There comes a point of no return as far as bringing the judgement of God down upon a nation is concerned, or to put it the other way round, when a nation becomes exposed to the enemy's activity against it. The sin of Damascus and Gaza was to treat people like 'things' both in war and in their economy. Tyre and Edom broke covenants of brotherhood between nations and cities. Ammon and Moab abused the weak and the needy for no reason. In Amos 2:1 an example of Moab's abuse is cited: they are under judgement because they destroyed the King of Edom's bones. God does not judge them for actually killing the king because he was indeed an evil man, but they were judged for what they did with his body after he was dead. God does have norms for justice, and these points of His care for persons are vital.

We see these norms in other places in Scripture. We can presume that the temptations which Jesus faced in the wilderness reveal Satan's most strategic weapons against the human race. So it is interesting to notice that these temptations concern the human appetite, use of power, and tendency to operate in terms of position and status. These are ultimately the most demonic foundations: to put human appetites first, to abuse other people by the use of power, and to want to tread on other people by exercising position and status.

I have already touched upon the Canaanites: the judgement of the Lord fell upon that nation at the point where its people were actually enshrining and worshipping immorality and the occult in their religion and culture – it was at the heart of their national life. The first chapter of Romans shows us at what point the Lord takes His hand off a people and it is evident that impurity, deception, immorality, lawlessness and death are the signs of God's judgement.

In the end what corporate sin does is to give more and more place to the enemy. The enemy wants to thieve, to kill and to destroy, and the result of these tactics is that ultimately a spirit of death and of murder is released across a nation. This is what needs to be dealt with.

It is obvious that like Damascus and Gaza in Amos' day, Britain has also treated people like things in both war and economics. Like Tyre and Edom we have broken covenants of brotherhood between nations and cities, and like Ammon and Moab we have abused the weak and the needy for no reason. At no time has this been more true than in our colonial history. It is our purpose in this book to focus attention on the sins of Britain during the colonial era, exploring significant antecedents in our earlier history which gave rise to it, and tracing some of the more recent national sins which have ensued.

A key area that needs to be addressed is the ongoing significance of nations today. Some Christians have felt that there is really only one new nation since Christ's coming and that the verse in Revelation which speaks of *'every tribe and tongue and people and nation'* (Revelation 14:6) allows us to jump over national identities. When this view is taken, the suggestion of John Dawson and others that nations have redemptive gifts [2] today is neatly side-stepped. Recently, while reading Genesis, the weakness of this argument has been brought home to me. I first noted that Abraham was

promised that he would be the 'father of many nations'.
Then I realised that his promise passed only through Isaac.
Until then I had always assumed that it was fulfilled also
through the other sons of Abraham and Isaac. But this
cannot be the case if it is part of the covenant promise. This
is not to devalue the significance before God of those nations
outside the Old Testament Covenant, but simply to point out
that they were not the fulfilment of God's promise to
Abraham. This becomes clearest of all when the promise is
passed on through Joseph's sons by Jacob at the end of his
life. It makes it 100 per cent clear for me that this father of
nations' promise was not fulfilled in Old Testament days, for
by Joseph's time all the non-Jewish relatives of Abraham,
Isaac and Jacob were established. Yet the promise was still
being proclaimed. For the rest of the promise to be fulfilled it
was necessary for Jesus to come. It is He who is the father of
many nations – the father of those nations that proceed
from the remnant of the nations of the earth as they turn to
Him. This is surely what the prophets refer to when they
speak of a remnant of the Philistines, of Egypt and so on (e.g.
Zechariah 9:6–7). This insight of course greatly increases the
importance and understanding of reconciliation between
nations and the role of the Church in each nation that
makes up together the one new humanity of Ephesians
2:14–22.

One of the most clear and helpful passages of Scripture on
the reality of corporate guilt and how to deal with it is found
in 2 Samuel 21:1. This deals with a period of famine in the
reign of King David and tells of how he *sought the presence of
the Lord.*

> '...*And the Lord said, "It is for Saul and his bloody house,
> because he put the Gibeonites to death."* '

The account goes on to describe how David consulted with
the surviving Gibeonites and made atonement by hanging
seven sons of Saul's house. Several significant points can be
drawn from this passage. The first is general, yet extremely
radical. A sin committed a generation ago by someone now
dead, breaking a covenant made five hundred years ago,
can bring a contemporary famine on a nation. If this can be

true physically and literally, it can certainly be the case spiritually. This has far-reaching implications when applied to the history of a nation like England.

The passage goes on to tell of how Rizpah, the mother of two of those who were hung, protected their bodies:

> '... *from the beginning of harvest until it rained on them from the sky; and she allowed neither the birds of the sky to rest on them by day nor the beasts of the field by night.*'
>
> (2 Samuel 21:10)

It further recounts how as a result David honoured the bones of Saul and Jonathan by retrieving them from the men of Jabesh-gilead who had stolen them away from the battleground where they had fallen. He then buried them together with the bones of Saul's descendants who had been hanged and gave them all a proper burial in the family grave in Zola. The Scriptures conclude:

> '... *after that God was moved by entreaty for the land.*'
>
> (2 Samuel 21:14)

I suggest that the following four conclusions can also be drawn from this incident:

1. Confession followed by atonement can lift the guilt from a nation or people.

2. Viewed from the New Testament perspective we can see that the cross of Jesus fulfils the need for atonement and it is no longer necessary for representatives of the guilty to be physically punished.

3. Intercession by the representatives of the guilty (as made by Rizpah who fought off predators throughout the whole process) can protect the vulnerable representatives of the guilty while the truth is being uncovered and identificational repentance is being made.[3]

4. Those in spiritual authority need to make sure that a proper end is brought to the exercise of repentance and atonement, and proper honour is shown to the guilty (as demonstrated by giving them a decent burial, particularly including the bones of Saul himself).

It is impossible to start chasing through history trying to find a list of all the situations where we have broken God's justice norms and brought God's judgement upon ourselves. That would take the rest of our lives and it would prevent us from getting on with the work of the kingdom. But in the same way as the Holy Spirit homes in on an individual's life, as Jesus did with the woman at the well, so He places His finger on the crucial factors in our history, which when dealt with will lead to the greater release of the Holy Spirit into our nation, and greater blessings to those nations against which we have sinned.

Notes

1 Regal Books, 1994, chs. 6–11.
2. By 'redemptive gift' we are referring to our belief that each nation has a particular positive contribution or gift to bring as a blessing to the family of nations. It is often the opposite of what has been perceived in the way it has acted towards other nations.
3. When Brian and I admitted and repented for the genocidal behaviour of the British towards the Australian Aboriginals we were dependent on the intercessors present to protect both us and the Aboriginals from the justified extreme anger or revenge that they might have been tempted to vent on us.

Chapter 3

Rule Britannia

Rule Britannia, Britannia rules the waves,
Britain never, never, never shall be slaves.[1]

On the last night of the Proms, in a great splash of patriotism, of flag waving and cheering, six thousand people give expression to a burst of national pride. It is the climax not only of that one night but of the complete summer concert season at London's prestigious Royal Albert Hall. These annual scenes have become a national institution, full of tradition, nostalgia and sentiment. But how meaningful are they really?

The name Britannia once captured the proud hopes of our nation. A picture of this national heroine – bearing a striking similarity to the statue of the goddess Minerva on Liverpool's town hall – used to be stamped on all our coins. It was the name the Romans gave to these islands, the name Sir Winston Churchill recalled in his victory speech at the end of the Second World War, 'Advance Britannia. The war is won'.

The singing of 'Rule Britannia' is almost all that is left as a reminder of a nearly-forgotten period of power and glory for Britain. It was the time of the spread of the British Empire, the time when we did rule the waves as the world's leading maritime power.

At that time, from about the sixteenth century onwards, the English pioneer spirit was at its highest and, some would say, its best. It was the age of adventure, of pushing the boundaries of understanding; it was the age of discovery.

It was the Elizabethan period, with Elizabeth I the first monarch of a Protestant Britain. In Britain the Reformation had been initiated by Henry VIII, who did not like being under the thumb of Rome and the Church, for his own political and sexual ends. His six marriages would never have been tolerated by the Roman Church.

It was also the age of piracy on the high seas, of galleons laden with treasure, of forays to the West Indies and India; an age of slavery, with mass exportation of negroes from Africa to the West Indies, and exploitation of them by their white masters. As a nation we became power-hungry. Like civilisations before, we sought to subdue peoples, destroy cultures, and impose our own culture and control on as much of the world as we could.

For the next one hundred and fifty years new lands were being discovered and pioneers battled the elements to take the gospel 'to the uttermost parts of the earth'. But those who accompanied those first missionaries were often more interested in wealth and power, and so the message of the gospel was frequently compromised.

In this examination we want to give thanks to God for all the good that has flowed from right motivation. We want to honour men and women like William Carey, David Livingstone, Mary Slessor, William Wilberforce, Lord Brisbane, the Wesleys and George Whitefield. We are thankful for righteous men and women who went out from these shores, taking many good and civilising influences along with them, but we must not and cannot ignore the negative factors. Sin is sin. It should not be ignored or swept under the carpet, but faced, acknowledged, confessed, turned from and appropriately dealt with. In each of the chapters that follow we turn our attention to the many corners of the world where our historic actions have left a legacy of bad feeling, of revenge, hatred, fear and of opposition to the gospel.

A few days before we started writing this book, a member of the National Team of the Lydia Fellowship International telephoned me. 'We've been praying for years for the nations and for the gospel to flow out again from our land. But we've seen so little response,' she said. Then she asked, 'When are we going to do something about our appalling history as a nation during our Empire era? Surely God can't answer our prayers until our national sin is confessed?'

We know that this is precisely what God has been saying to us. Neither of us are historians, but we know that God has been saying, 'Deal with the sins of your forefathers.'

> *'Stand by the ways and see and ask for the ancient*
> *paths,*
> *Where the good way is, and walk in it.'* (Jeremiah 6:16)

God has led us to make many public acts of confession of corporate sin, asking for forgiveness from the Christian leaders of nations England has sinned against. But we feel that we are only at the start. We need more leaders who will feel the pain of the heart of God over what His people (and our forebears) have tolerated or committed, and who will be prepared to stand in the gap.

We must, however, face the question of whether we are talking about the sins of the Church or of the nation. Some would want to make a distinction between the wrong which is purposefully encouraged and initiated by the Church, and that which is a product of political decisions and international tensions. The question is made ever more complex when the Church is inextricably linked with the State.

Church identification with the State has been an issue since the time of Constantine in the fourth century. Having originated in the Orthodox Church of the East, it later emerged in Western Catholic countries. This tendency accelerated in many nations in the Protestant era following the Reformation. Sir Fred Catherwood has pointed out that:

> 'It was Protestants who, in winning the reformation of the church, accidentally destroyed the unity of Christendom. In this fight the Reformers needed the protection of their national princes. So the Lutheran churches became the churches of Saxony, of Sweden, Denmark and Norway; the Calvinist churches became the churches of Switzerland, the Netherlands and Scotland; and the unique Church of England made its national sovereign its head in place of the pope. It was Protestants who began to identify church with state and give to the state a loyalty which Norman kings had never received from Welsh and Saxon subjects.'[2]

Later, in the nineteenth century, as the Christian faith began to decline, people began to switch their allegiance from the cross to the flag. Consequently today, in some of our 'religious wars' it is hard to distinguish between State and Church. In Northern Ireland, for example, Protestants rally under the Union Jack, Catholics under the Irish tricolour. In the conflict in the Balkans, Catholics rallied together under the Croatian flag, and received the blessing of Catholic priests before going into war, while Orthodox people rallied under the Serbian flag and received the blessing of Orthodox priests. Bosnian Muslims imported those schooled in guerrilla warfare from Afghanistan, Iran and other recent Islamic trouble spots, learning from the fundamentalist approach that was often their motivation for Jihad.

In Britain, because the sovereign is still the Head of the Church, we cannot really make the distinction between what is State sin and what is Church sin. We cannot excuse ourselves as Christians from the guilt associated with so many of our atrocities. We are in part responsible when the State passes legislation which contravenes God's laws – particularly when we do nothing to oppose that legislation. By allowing (through our silence) the breaking of covenants and treaties, and the introduction of laws which are unrighteous and unjust, we acquiesce to our nation's sins. We are part of the nation that is responsible.

For example, the repeal of the Witchcraft Act in 1951, which went unchallenged, has taken away all restraint, allowing the floodgates of paganism through occult practice, occult materials and occult influences to affect our entire nation. The Abortion Act of 1967, allowing the termination of the life of the unborn for social as well as medical reasons, came into being with opposition from only a minority in society. It has resulted in the legally induced deaths throughout England and Wales of 4.7 million children (1997 figures)[3] in the place which is intended to be the safest for them – the womb. It is estimated that one in five established pregnancies also end in abortion.[4] Consequently the unspoken grief and guilt for these premature deaths (with no proper burial for them) is carried by approximately one in five women in England and Wales. The blood guilt is huge!

Muslim nations have followed in the footsteps of Christian ones. Islam is indistinguishable from national politics. In countries where Islam is the predominant religion, the nation becomes an Islamic state, and many political decisions taken are motivated by Islamic laws and dogma.

So as we look at Britain's Empire, we have to recognise that it spread during the Protestant era. Protestant missions to bring the gospel to the unconverted made no distinction about religion. Any nation that was not Protestant was considered valid for missionary endeavour. Initially the drive was to any 'pagan' nation. Where the Empire became established, and with it the protection of the Colonial Office, there missionary work increased and became established too. Later still, Catholic countries were included.

From the age of nine I lived and went to school in Plymouth, where Sir Francis Drake played bowls before going out to defeat the Spanish Armada. *The Mayflower* set sail from there for America. Drake, like many of these early pioneers, was a Protestant. In all my history lessons about Drake, however, I never remember hearing about his faith – only his exploits. His belief was that God worked through him and gave him protection, so that he could encounter the most dangerous of situations. He also knew that taking on the Spanish involved taking on Catholicism which was seeking to reimpose its will on the breakaway Protestant nations. He received the 'blessing' of Protestant Elizabeth I in his war against Catholic Philip II of Spain. Philip of Spain was seen as the agent of Catholicism in its resistance by force to what was regarded as Protestant heresy.

The point that we need to make is that during the establishment of the Empire we were bringing civilisation to the uncivilised and Christianity to the unevangelised. But the real distinction between the two was never made or understood and the result has been that much of the legacy from the Empire period is seen as a legacy not just of State but also of Church.

On the one hand we have taken blessing to the nations. Medicine, education, communications, trade, more modern means of transport. These advancements, among many others, have been perceived as a blessing. We have also taken the gospel to every nation where we had influence. The tragic reality is, however, that we have also been oppressors. We have viewed other races as inferior. We have belittled others' humanity. Instead of acting like a father nation, we have more often acted as a despot. Driven by a will to rule, our desire to express our superiority sometimes culminated in flagrant violence and corruption. As a result the legacy we have left around the world is often viewed in negative terms.

We like to remember the good we have done. Others remember the bad.

As we have taken a long hard look at ourselves, we have had to ask the question, 'Where did this spirit of control and rulership come from?' Christian leaders in other parts of the world have tried to define our nation's redemptive gift. Pieter Bos from Holland considers our destiny to be a 'humorous father' – pleasant and fatherlike to other nations, with a keen sense of humour. Instead, this gift has been corrupted until we have become a father who acts cynically out of self-interest. Others think we have a gift of 'majesty' – rulership with authority and grace. But that, too, has been corrupted. Where did it all go wrong?

As we explore further in chapter 14, we need to try to understand who we are as a nation. The will to rule and the desire for empire have come from the English – **not** the Scots, Welsh or Irish. Yet, it is hard for most of us as English people to acknowledge our 'Englishness'.

The sins we committed against the nations of our empire were basically the very same sins we committed against our own neighbouring nations. In fact they were perpetrated against even our own young as, for example, in the abandonment of child convicts discussed in the chapter on Australia, and the abuse of children in industry during the Industrial Revolution! Having brought them up in a system of intimidation, cruelty, fear and control, it is no wonder that they then went out and acted in much the same way towards people of other nations. We have surely been guilty of the intimidation and abuse of them too. Scripture warns fathers about this:

> *'Fathers, do not exasperate your children ... and masters, treat your slaves in the same way. Do not threaten them, since*

you know that He who is both their Master and yours is in
heaven, and there is no favouritism with Him.'

(Ephesians 6:4, 9 NIV)

Many will argue that it is hard for us to judge history from
our perspective hundreds of years later. Conditions were
harsher then. There was more violence and a climate of ill-
will. Society was polarised between the rich ruling classes
and the poor and destitute. There was a lack of education and
therefore much ignorance. But there was still the Church,
there was still the Bible, and above all, there was still the God
of Love who was believed in and preached.

An article in *Third Way* Magazine published in February
1998 discussed questions about England and the English. In
it Richard Wilkins writes:

'England has enjoyed centuries of domination of the
British Isles, and as the heart of an empire has wielded
great power over subject peoples on five continents. Its
former economic and imperial expansion made it
responsible for the experiences of hundreds of millions
of people. Its imposition of its own social hierarchies
resulted in neglect, oppression and inhumanity which
the English must not forget. English Christians must
work quickly to build penitence into the growing
national self-awareness.'

We agree! The English have not had an Anglo-Saxon
monarch for nine hundred years. The Anglo-Saxons were
succeeded by the Danes and Anglo-Normans, and since 1066
we have been ruled by the Norman-French, Welsh, Scottish
and German. Kings ruled and princes decreed justice. We
need to remember that it is only in comparatively recent
times that governments have wielded more power, and the
monarchy less.

The English are a nation descended from immigrants, and
as rough and bloodthirsty a group of nations as they could
be: the Anglo-Saxons, the Vikings, the Normans and before
that, the ancient Britons and the Romans. This will to rule, to
subdue, to control, to invade, to pillage and to conquer has
become embedded in our history, from whatever source we

may have come. What evil spirits have been brought here by our forefathers and have found their home in the development of this nation, and in the attitudes and lifestyle of succeeding generations?

The term 'British' emerged only after the Act of Union with Scotland in 1707. Before that there was a clear national distinction and identity. We believe that we, as English people, need to acknowledge this distinction again. Not because we wish to see a form of nationalism develop, but because we need to acknowledge our sin. In the process of doing that we may discover a new national identity. Surely that would be an appropriate way to begin a new millennium, as we give back to Scotland, Wales and Northern Ireland a measure of self-rule and government. We may even have to find a new flag, a new realism about our weakness and a new humility in taking our place in the family of nations – both here and in the global village. 'Rule Britannia', sung so lustily by supporters of the England Team at international football matches, or by the crowds on the last night of the Proms, is no longer appropriate. In fact it is becoming obnoxious.

Notes

1. From 'Rule Britannia' by James Thomson, 1740.
2. Sir Fred Catherwood, *Pro-Europe?* (IVP, 1991), p. 41.
3. Government figures provided by the Care Trust.
4. John Wyatt, *Matters of Life and Death: Today's Healthcare Dilemmas in the Light of Christian Faith* (IVP, 1998).

Chapter 4

Crusades and Crusaders

By all accounts and by all yardsticks of morally wrong actions, the Crusades stand out in the whole of human history. For nine hundred years they have been a blot on the history of the world, and particularly of the Christian Church. The manner in which they were undertaken, the reasons why they were undertaken, the fact that they were undertaken – they were all wrong. Wrong by any human standard, and certainly wrong by God's standards.

Even more reprehensible is the fact that they were initiated and executed by those who claimed to be Christians. To take the sign of the cross and turn it into a sword to kill, maim and desecrate is utterly appalling. But that is what happened.

Have you ever wondered why it seems the conflicts around the world centre on the clash between those people who would call themselves Muslims, Christians or Jews? The horrors of the Holocaust, fundamentalist terrorism, the Gulf War, slaughter of Muslims and the tensions over Israel are all well-chronicled expressions of the continuing conflict between the three great monotheistic faiths.

Of course many are called Jews, Muslims or Christians in name only. Their actions do not necessarily represent the feelings or beliefs of true followers, nor of the main tenets of their respective faiths. Yet the world looking on does not see the many different expressions of belief within each faith, but judges the whole faith by the actions of one extremist group.

In Bosnia, Chechnya, Algeria and other Muslim areas, we find Muslims protecting themselves or lashing out against what they believe is the 'last crusade' being waged by the

West against Islam. Their understanding is that this crusade is not being fought so much with swords and soldiers, but with the more powerful weapons of ideas, economics, media and culture.

Many Muslims look at Hollywood films, MTV,[1] drugs, drink and pornography and see it as the output of Christian civilisation. Some associate the tolerance of free sex among young people with Christianity, and this becomes a further hindrance to them ever exploring the Christian faith, or being sympathetic towards it. As the popular culture of the West spreads, Muslims raise their defences to fend off this direct attack against their cultural and religious identity.

On the other side of the picture, in Sudan and other parts of North Africa and in Asia, Muslim governments and fundamentalist parties seek to spread their way of life by the use of force against Christian, Jewish or animist minorities. In Pakistan and Iran, non-Muslim people live in fear of the consequences of Muslim law, including the death sentence for blaspheming against the Muslim faith. Within every faith there are of course large numbers of faithful believers who harbour no animosity. In spite of all the conflict, many Muslims today have a genuine respect for and interest in the person of Jesus Christ. What they and so many Jews distrust is 'Christianity'. This distrust has various roots, but the tap root can be found in events which took place nine hundred years ago.

The Crusades

Between 1096 and 1250 there were a number of separate Crusades to regain Jerusalem for Christian pilgrims, which necessitated fighting against Muslims and Jews. The word 'crusade' has its origins in these expeditions and one dictionary has the following definitions:

1.   Any of several medieval military expeditions made by Europeans to recover the Holy Land from the Muslims.
2.   A war instigated by the Church for alleged religious ends.

Christian leaders meeting in Korea in October 1993 covenanted never again to use this word in a Christian context because of its worst associations. In addition, they agreed to encourage Christian organisations with the word 'crusade' in their name to change it.

By the end of the tenth century the spread of Islam had all but stopped and a comparatively stable state of affairs existed between Muslims, Jews and Christians, with the latter able to make pilgrimages to Jerusalem, which at that stage was under Muslim rule.

This comparative stability came to an end, however, with the aggressive expansion of the Seljuk Turks, a race of nomadic shepherds from the steppes of Central Asia. They had been converted to Islam as they moved westwards and by 1055 ran a huge empire which stretched from Central Asia and southern Russia to the northern borders of Syria.

The Turks inevitably rubbed up against the eastern borders of what was then the greatest Christian power-base in the world – the Byzantine Empire – with its capital in Constantinople (now Istanbul). In 1071, the Turks defeated the Byzantine army at the Battle of Manzikert, leaving the greatest city in the world vulnerable and weakened.

The Turks had also started ambushing parties of Christian pilgrims on their way to Jerusalem. The various routes to the Holy City had been relatively safe up till then, and these sudden attacks alarmed the European Christians who placed great importance on pilgrimages.

The Christian world at this stage was split in two. In the middle of the eleventh century the Emperor and Bishop of Constantinople had excommunicated the Bishop of Rome (the Pope), who in turn excommunicated them. There was no longer one Church.

[The seeds of this split had been sown three hundred years earlier in a secret deal in Paderborn, Germany, between Charlemagne and Pope Leo III, who later crowned Charlemagne King of the Roman Empire. This had two effects. It brought the papacy into conflict with the prevailing Byzantine Empire and it further reinforced the marrying of secular and religious powers. Charlemagne's methodology was to convert people to Christianity by force: refusing to be baptised carried the death penalty. On one day 4500 reluctant Saxons were executed for not worshipping the right God.]

With the Byzantine Empire at threat now from the Turks, the Emperor Alexius was forced to swallow his pride and send a request from Constantinople to Pope Urban II in Rome for help. This cry for help was a perfect opportunity for Pope Urban II to regain some influence over Constantinople and also fulfil his obligation to protect the rights of Christendom.

On 27 November 1095 thousands gathered outside the cathedral in Clermont Ferrand in France to hear Pope Urban's message. At this great gathering he called Western Christendom to take up arms and liberate the Holy Land. With the Pope's message stirring his listeners to fever pitch, they shouted, 'God wills it', and began to sew the sign of the cross on their tunics. Within months thousands had started the long trek eastwards, anxious to bear the sword in the name of Jesus Christ and to free Jerusalem from the Muslim infidel.

One popular slogan announced 'We shall slay for God's love'. Every death on either side would please God. Christian crusaders who died would go to heaven – the Pope had promised that – and every death of an 'infidel' would bring glory to God's name.

St Bernard added his own endorsement, 'A Christian glories in the death of a Muslim because Christ is glorified. The liberality of God is revealed in the death of a Christian, because he is led out to his reward.'[2]

'So powerful was the saving grace of going on crusade that St Bernard urged "Murderers, rapists, adulterers, perjurers, and all other criminals" to join the expedition. However holy the motive, it sounded much like an invitation to violence.'[3]

And so it was. The First Crusade was conducted not by a disciplined army of soldiers, but by a mobile riot of thousands of peasants, complete with their families. They were dominated by superstitions, easily manipulated and desperate to do something that would smooth the road to heaven.

The first and second wave of Crusaders murdered, raped and plundered their way up the Rhine and down the Danube, as they headed for Jerusalem. They especially targeted Jewish communities, and thousands of Jews were massacred – particularly in the German towns of Cologne, Mainz, Worms and Spier. Many Jewish scholars refer to this as the First Holocaust. This was to become almost a traditional start to every expedition eastwards.

As the Crusaders proceeded down the Danube, it wasn't just Jews who came in for their terrifying attention. Communities of Orthodox Christians were devastated too, with their women raped, their men murdered, their churches desecrated and their icons destroyed.

But it was against Muslims and Jews that the Crusaders' main attention was focused. In June 1099, nearly four years after the first call to arms, the Crusaders, including the second wave of knights and professional soldiers, reached the prize, Jerusalem. The Holy City had been governed by Arab Muslims for many generations but was also inhabited by Christians and Jews who lived as second-class citizens alongside their Arab masters. As the Crusaders approached, all the Christians were expelled from the city in preparation for the inevitable siege.

On 15 July, after weeks of stale-mate, the Crusaders finally breached the northern wall and broke into the city. They slaughtered men, women and children throughout the day and well into the night. As the sun rose, the marauders discovered about 6,000 Jews who had fled to the synagogue for refuge. They set the synagogue alight and burned them alive. The surviving Muslims had fled to the Mosque of al Aqsa in the south-eastern quarter of the city. The Crusaders broke down the doors and slaughtered an estimated 30,000 Muslims.

One commentator on these events wrote:

> 'With drawn swords our people ran throughout the city; nor did they spare anyone, not even those pleading for mercy. If you had been there, your feet would have been stained up to the ankles with blood. What more shall I tell? Not one of them was allowed to live. They did not spare the women or children. The horses waded in blood up to their knees, nay up to the bridle. It was a just and wonderful judgement of God.'[4]

The result of this slaughter and the next two centuries of warfare, intrigue and betrayal convinced the Muslims that there was no greater evil than these barbaric Christian hordes from feudal Europe. For two centuries the occupation of Jerusalem and of Constantinople changed hands. Each time Muslims gained possession the Christian Church's Crusaders would mount a fresh crusade to liberate Jerusalem.

Toward the end of the thirteenth century the Muslims were finally successful in expelling the last of the European invaders. The legacy of that period was a deep mutual hatred.

The Spiritual Tenor of the Middle Ages

At the time of the Crusades, the official Church had become corrupt and politically motivated. Apart from a tiny elite, people were illiterate and even if they could read, there was no access to a Bible or any scriptural teaching.

It was an age of superstition and magic, where visions, signs and wonders were claimed by many. The masses' only source of knowledge about God was whatever the corrupt and greedy clergy decided to teach.

The Church taught that acts of penance, indulgences and pilgrimages were the only means of escaping the tortures of purgatory and entering the bliss of heaven. Because the emphasis on pilgrimage and relic worship was so strong, the Church felt a responsibility to keep the routes to Jerusalem open.

In order to ignite the fire of the Crusades, the Pope was forced to take existing theology about violence and warfare and turn it on its head. Until this time a Christian soldier was required to do penance for any violence he committed in order to reduce the time he would spend in purgatory before going to heaven. Violence was considered a necessary evil, but nevertheless still evil.

Popes Gregory VII and Urban II changed that. They said that an act of warfare against the infidel, i.e. Muslims, was in itself an act of penance, and any Christian who lost his life in the process of killing Muslims would go straight to heaven. Many Crusaders extended this concept to include killing Jews too. With many people facing what they believed could be countless years in purgatory, it is no wonder that tens of thousands willingly gave themselves to the cause of killing the infidel.

Our Response

We can imagine that these facts might lead many Protestants to take the view that because these atrocities were carried out by Catholics, Catholicism is apostate and it is therefore a Catholic problem, not a Protestant one. But God says:

> *'Since you did not hate bloodshed, bloodshed will pursue you.'*
> (Genesis 9:6)

The cycle gets repeated in successive generations because the problem is not addressed. Something has to change.

We would want to say strongly that because these barbaric acts were committed in the name of Christ by those who, for better or worse, were regarded as our Christian forebears, we cannot escape the importance and implications of doing something to set the record straight. Something needs to be done before our fellow human beings and before God. We may, in retrospect, not agree with what happened so long ago in history and we may want to disassociate ourselves from it. That is a valid response, but we don't change anything by absolving ourselves from responsibility.

We may, on the other hand, wish to engage in a sackcloth and ashes equivalent of covering ourselves with shame, apologising and asking for forgiveness – not only for what happened during the Crusades, but also for all the unrighteous acts and hateful attitudes that have continued to characterise relationships between Christians and Jews or Muslims. The Reconciliation Walks from Western Europe to Jerusalem following the original Crusade routes – nine hundred years on – are significant expressions of such sorrow. But there needs to be more.

In Spain every town or major village has its annual fiesta. The whole population prepares all year for a week of festivity and a tax is compulsorily deducted from all wage earners to pay for the costs. In these fiestas however, the two major themes that are regularly re-enacted are 'The Moors versus the Christians', or 'The Crusades'. In this way the memory of history and the antagonisms towards Muslims are constantly reinforced.

However, an apology from King Juan Carlos of Spain a few

years ago went a long way to healing Spain's past. He publically apologised for the way Spain had treated the Jews through the Crusades, and later through the Spanish Inquisition. Yet sadly, nothing has changed in the main streets and market places of Spanish towns.

In Korea in October 1993 we were both involved in a dramatic public act of renunciation of the effects of the Crusades. As we stood with fellow leaders from European nations involved in the Crusades, we apologised to Jewish leaders present. We confessed the pain of what Christians had done in the name of Christ. We broke the Toledo Sword – symbol of the Crusaders' weapons of destruction – and we prayed to break the Crusading spirit over Christendom. We asked God to reverse what had happened in history, so that instead of violence, there would be peace; instead of death, we could bring life; instead of taking, we would have opportunities to give to them. We asked for open doors for Christ's love into the Jewish and Muslim nations, and we prayed for the blood of Jesus to cover all our sin and to break its power.

This is only a tiny part of the repentance process! However, we believe that as more and more Christians begin to humble themselves before God and confess the terrible sins of the past, an atmosphere of conciliation and of reconciliation can come into being. And that can only mean good news for human relationships, good news for the human race and good news for the poor![5]

Notes

1. Music television.
2. Norman Daniel, *Islam and the West: The Making of an Image* (Oneworld Publications, 1997), p. 113.
3. Bamber Gascoigne, *The Christians* (Jonathan Cape, 1987), p. 113.
4. Norman Cohn, *Pursuit of the Millennium* (OUP, 1990), quoted in Gascoigne, *The Christians*, p. 113.
5. Our thanks to Lynn Green who has researched this subject and has allowed us to quote extensively from his pamphlet promoting the Reconciliation Walk.

Chapter 5

From the Pacific to Africa

As an introduction to thinking about Africa, I want to begin outside the continent with lessons I have learnt in the Pacific Islands. In May 1995 Ed Silvoso was invited by church leaders to conduct a city-reaching conference in Hawaii. I was among those he invited to join him on our return from the GCOWE conference of that year, held once again in Seoul, Korea. I was keen to participate as I knew that the conference was likely to involve some identificational repentance over the sins perpetuated against the Island peoples. Hawaii once had the largest Church in the world, was more than 90 per cent Christian and had a wonderful Christian queen. However, second-generation missionary families stole the nation's lands by deception and ultimately worked for the overthrow of the queen and the surrender of native Hawaiian independence into European hands.

My involvement with the Pacific Islands dates back to the early eighties when I was Development Secretary for Pacific Students for Christ, seconded by the International Fellowship of Evangelical Students and based at the University of the South Pacific. Back then I had sensed the need to apologise for Britain's treatment of the Islanders during the colonial era. Probably nowhere was this more obviously wrong than in Fiji. The native Fijians never rose to the British encouragement to reorganise their society on lines more economically productive to Britain. Finding the Fijians unwilling to develop and work sugar cane plantations, South Indians were deceived into coming as indentured labourers who were really scarcely more than slaves and whose pay and conditions were so appalling that it was most unlikely that they would ever be able to take up their supposed right to return to India in the event that they didn't like the situation when they got there (see also chapter 6). The result is a nation divided on ethnic, socio-cultural and religious lines, a situation worsened by the romantic attempts of subsequent colonial governors to safeguard the Fijian way of life by seeing to it that the freehold of the land remained in native Fijian control. In the course of time the descendants of the Indian indentured labourers made up nearly half the population but were denied freehold land rights.

My attempts to apologise were countered by polite discouragement. People were grateful to have been under British rule rather than a colonial power such as the French, whom they regarded as even more oppressive in their involvement in the region. At the time I didn't know what else to do, not having the biblical understanding that the Holy Spirit has been giving us in recent years. But it did press home to me the **European** nature of the problem. In many ways the sins of Britain typify the sins of Europe and of the European peoples of which we are a part.

It was a great privilege then, at the Hawaii conference, to be able to stand for Europe, the cradle of European peoples, alongside descendants of those original American missionary families as we confessed the sins of our fathers and received the forgiveness of the representative leaders of the Pacific Island peoples.

As I began to turn my attention to Africa I discovered that nowhere is it more true than in this continent that the sins of the colonial era are the sins of the whole of Europe. At the Berlin Congress of 1884–5 leaders of the major European powers of the time divided up Africa among themselves simply on the basis of where they could prove their ability to maintain military authority. In 1870 Europeans controlled only 10 per cent of the African continent, by 1900 90 per cent of it was apportioned, carved up on paper with little regard for geography or for the African peoples.[1] Two decades of the bloody mopping up of any African resistance followed. It was true in Africa, as my Pacific friends had hinted from their own experience, that French military strategy was probably the most aggressive. But examples of British military violence abound. In the conquest of Sudan in 1898, for example, over 20,000 Sudanese were killed in fighting. The battle for supremacy in Southern Africa culminated in the Boer War of 1900–2 where approximately 27,000 Afrikaner women and children and 20,000 of their Black African employees died in the concentration camps which we established.

At the 1884–5 Congress the European Powers appointed themselves the legal arbiters for the appropriation of African territory. Strictly speaking the apportioning of Africa followed bit by bit – but the right to do it was agreed then. The *UNESCO General History of Africa* states that:

'... there is no precedent in world history where a group of states in one continent felt justified in talking about the sharing and occupation of the territory of another continent in such a bold manner. This is the major significance of the conference for African history.'[2]

We ask the question, 'What possessed the Europeans to think and act in this way?' It is not our purpose here to comment politically: our purpose is to assess these actions biblically from the point of view of the judgement of God. Certainly during the period that followed the Congress of Berlin, people were treated like things, treaties were made and broken, and the poor and needy were abused. The *UNESCO General History of Africa* continues:

'An examination of the political treaties suggests the conclusion that some of them were legally indefensible, some morally bankrupt, while others were procured legally. Nevertheless they were essentially political acts defensible only in the context of European positive law which saw force as the basis of all law.'[3]

The incredible audacity with which the European powers treated the native Africans with almost complete disregard between 1600 and the 1970s can be seen as involving a mixture of economic greed and pseudo-intellectual notions of superiority. If the Atlantic slave trade in West Africa was driven by the former, Cecil Rhodes' adventures in South Africa were bolstered with more sophistication by the latter.

Darwinism represents one of the pinnacles of modernism. According to its tenets, natural selection supports a conclusion that those nations and cultures with the most power have the right to be the most powerful because they have risen furthest from the primeval swamps. So in Africa, by the time we reached the last decades of the nineteenth century, there was an assumption (most evident among the British) that our colonial enterprises were in part at least a humanitarian expedition to benefit Africans with our racial superiority.

Most enlightened Europeans would feel a sense of shame today if we were thought to have attitudes of racial superiority. We have learned to appreciate the richness and simple joy of African cultures, as well as their enormous capacity for intellectual achievements. A century ago it would have been commonplace to consider Africans subhuman. This is serious sin and the very opposite of biblical teaching on how we should treat other nations.

In this climate, the European powers behaved very differently from one another. For some, the concept of African inferiority bred gross brutality. In south-west Africa there are stories of a German party which massacred over 400 bushmen for sport in what is now Namibia. The Portuguese, literally forced to abandon their trade in slaves, continued to operate indentured labour on the islands of Sao Tome and Principe until well into this century. A recent visitor encountered a missionary who had personally seen a group of Angolans run into the bush when he produced a rope from his Land Rover. Within living memory their peoples had been captured and taken to the islands.

The British liked to appear more respectable and refused to tolerate such excesses. In our case, driven by missionary zeal for both the Christian gospel and our own economic weight, it was the use of 'diplomacy' that was used to dominate Africa. This often involved the deceiving of Africans, the making and breaking of treaties and the use of threats to our neighbours.

The Congress of Berlin is the best example of this. Because of British military and economic power at that time, we were able to squeeze the Portuguese out of the hinterland of the mouth of the Zambezi, to grab the Copperbelt from the Belgians in the south of Congo, to wrestle for control of the River Nile with all powers, and so it goes on. However, alongside the sin of treating Africa as a chattel rather than as land belonging to its own peoples, is the greater crime of dividing tribes.

In central Africa there is a wonderful tribe called the Lunda people. At the Congress of Berlin, dominated by an exclusively European agenda, tribal boundaries were not considered at all. Indeed, the policy was 'divide and rule' and there is much evidence that divisive tribalism as we often encounter it through the media today has been fuelled by colonial decisions.

As the lines of Africa were drawn, the border between British, Portuguese and Belgian colonies neatly divided the Lunda in three. For over a century now these people have been separated and treated as being from different nations. Even today, the legacy of colonialism forces the people of Lunda to think of themselves as Angolans, Congolese or Zambians. A visa is needed for a Lunda in Angola to visit a relative in Zambia.

Thankfully, in the Church all sorts of Lunda people are finding a new unity together, but elsewhere these divisions have caused ancient hatreds. For example, the bitter thirty years of Angolan civil war was fuelled by the division of tribes between the powers in its region. The notorious division between the Hutus and Tutsis as servant and ruling classes was actually designed as a means of control by the Belgian authorities.

The answer to our question as to what possessed the Europeans to act in this way is best answered using Jesus' temptations as our explanatory tool. In his overview of the various explanations G.N. Uzoigwe groups the many theories under three general headings: economics, psychology and prestige.[4] By psychology he basically means the psychology of dominance. The parallel with our earlier analysis in chapter 2 of Jesus' three temptations as being materialism, power and status is striking. These foundations are precisely the foundations of Satan's kingdom, which Jesus refused at the beginning of His ministry and died and rose again to overcome. It is impossible to avoid the conclusion that demonic strongholds were erected between Britain and Africa during those colonial days. It is our conviction that many still hold strong, that European nations in general and Britain in particular stand condemned over the fundamental basis of their colonial relationship with Africa and that we need to know from heaven the times and the places to deal with these issues as a matter of urgency.

In March 1997 I had the opportunity to visit South Africa, nearly one hundred years after the terrible British blood-letting of the Boer War. Until the AD 2000 Gideon's Army conference described in chapter 1, I had little or no know-ledge of either the scale of British atrocities in the Boer War nor its impact on Afrikaner people. But at that time Gerda Leithgob, an Afrikaner intercessor, came to me. She explained that she was moved by the Holy Spirit to confess the sin of apartheid to the native African intercessors at the conference on behalf of her people. However, she had discovered that she had no inner freedom to do this without first forgiving the British for their part in the deaths of so many of her ancestors and the apartheid system that grew out of the wounds that British genocide opened up. I gladly accepted to stand in for British sin, although I knew little or nothing of it before. But the moment I began to confess, waves of sorrow and guilt swept over me. I began to under-stand the spiritual reality of corporate sin and judgement. Although since then I have experienced it many times, the power of that first moment will stay with me. It was then that Gerda and I agreed that when God opened up the way I would come with an intercession team to South Africa, which I was eventually privileged to do in March 1997.

Several stories come to mind from those days of repent-ance, but perhaps the most striking was our visit to an elderly High Court judge who was a direct descendant of one of the first South African prime ministers of the apartheid era. As a result of our identificational repentance to him for the sins of Britain he surprised us all in coming, despite his infirm condition, to join in our repentance service at the famous Mothers and Children's memorial in Blomfontein, an event which saw many black South African leaders joining us to

witness our repentance to their white South African neighbours. Few if any of them had ever before set foot on what
was effectively Afrikaner hallowed ground. An illuminating
twist to the story came when I asked the judge if he could
shed any light on the source of the many Scottish names of
towns and landmarks in the surrounding countryside. I
particularly asked about the origins of the area known as
Glencoe. He quickly revealed that many of the white settlers
were Scots who left the highlands over the troubles with the
English and told us that he himself traced his ancestry to
the MacDonald clan baby smuggled out from the Glencoe
Massacre by his nurse in 1692. Once again the knock-on
effect of English oppression can be seen as his family became
the fathers of apartheid. This is the cycle that identificational
repentance can break through the blood of Christ!

Wonderful work has been done over the last few years to
locate key areas of European sin against Africa. We thank
God for the initiatives taken by African intercessors such as
Emeka Nwankpa, Gerda Leithgob, Langton Gatsi and John
Mulinde to name but a few and the identificational repentance of men and women such as the Welsh Dr Rhiannon
Lloyd, the Dutch Pieter Bos, the Swiss Michel von Allmen
and the English David Tidy and Chris Seaton. But we really
are only at the beginning of revelation and research and the
initial forays of intercessory action. As European leaders and
intercessors we have to move forward in repentance over
Africa as a matter of extreme urgency.

Spirits of violence and death have been resourced and
released which have played their part in the devastating
famines and tribal genocides of this century. If only the
revival in Rwanda and Burundi had been accompanied by a
proper biblical understanding of the nature of corporate sin
and the possibility of identificational repentance, the history
of relations between Hutus and Tutsis might have been a very
different story. A crevice has been opened up and in many
places left open between our continents which has given
spirits of death and murder space to operate. In my experience and relationships alone I know now of eighteen deaths
or martyrdoms in recent years strongly linked to both Britain
and Africa which are best explained in terms of this open

wound haunted by murderous spirits. I refer, for example, to the premature deaths of four young men known to me personally: one young man by drowning, one in an inexplicable road accident, one in a fall while prayer walking, and one from cancer – all of whom shared a link between Britain and Africa. I could give names and stories for all eighteen deaths, but I deliberately preserve their anonymity to avoid the emotions and controversies which would be stirred if I listed them. Not everyone would agree with my analysis, but I believe it stands.

Notes

1. Trevor Rowell, *Living Through History: the Scramble for Africa* (Batsford, 1986).
2. A. Adu Boaheu (ed.), (USA: Heinemann Lazif, 1985), p. 29.
3. Ibid., p. 34.
4. *UNESCO General History of Africa* Vol. VII (Heinemann, 1985), ch. 2.

Chapter 6

Conquering the Colonies

At school we used to be taught that the British colonial era was a glorious period of our history. It was the age of adventure, of pioneering, of exploring new worlds. We discovered that the world was round and not flat, that there were distant undiscovered lands with resources that were attractive, plentiful and worth exploiting. There were also peoples to be subdued and conquered: indigenous peoples, who were different in colour, language, religion and custom – people we regarded as primitive, uneducated, even subhuman.

Many of the early pioneers were idealists. The Americas were settled by religious separatists, fleeing from what they saw as 'the King's Church' – i.e., the State Church. They wanted to set up a true spiritual haven of truth and righteousness. But within a generation, forced to trade and subdue in order to survive, their ideals had altered to accommodate the need for commerce, for defence with arms, for imposing their beliefs and ideals on others in order to preserve their own 'purity'.

West Africa was first colonised by the Portuguese in the fifteenth century. By the middle of the sixteenth century, other colonial powers – like Spain, France, Britain, and Holland – had become involved. Here too it was trade that predominated: trade in gold, and in 'black ivory' – human beings. Historians estimate that at least thirty million Africans were exported from their homelands as slaves over more than three hundred years of slave trading.

The British trading ports of Bristol and Liverpool were key in the development of this pernicious slave trade. It has been asserted that the 'slave trade profits provided one of the main streams of that accumulation of capital in England which financed the Industrial Revolution'.[1] In fact much of our modern wealth is due to the exploitation of our former colonies. We made ourselves rich by keeping them poor.

Nowhere is this seen more starkly than in the West Indies. And perhaps nowhere is our reputation as corrupt and bloodstained as it is there.

When the explorers arrived in the West Indies they discovered the islands were inhabited by native Indians known as the Carib Indians. They were peaceful tribespeople but they were deeply suspicious and hostile towards the white invaders. Trouble came when it was discovered that the Carib Indians had access to gold. The explorers tried to buy it with beads, and for a while they succeeded but a chief soon got wise to the value being placed on the gold and the Indians began to refuse to hand over any more. Their refusal angered the invaders who deemed them to be a rebellious people. The Carib Indians refused to become the slaves of white masters and so, in the eyes of the interlopers, they had to be eliminated.

However, a labour force was needed to work the sugar and banana plantations for the benefit of Europeans. Having seen the slave trade in action in other parts of the world, in the days when Christopher Columbus discovered West Africa's Gold Coast, benefiting the Muslim and European nations, it appeared a natural progression for slaves from Africa to be taken to the West Indies and thousands of Africans were shipped to the islands. Unfortunately by this time these Africans were not only used to being slaves, but some of their own people had learned to engage in the trade themselves. Today in islands like Jamaica and Barbados, Afro-Caribbeans account for over 90 per cent of the population.

The Carib Indians became the victims of ethnic cleansing in order to make room for the islands' new workforce. They were rounded up, their women were raped and killed, and their men and children were forcibly marched into the sea until they drowned. In island after island the British, French and Spanish pirates and traders did the same. It was genocide.

Today very few Carib Indians exist. A small pocket escaped to the hills of Jamaica, some tribes fled to the interior of what is today Honduras, Guyana, Belize and the former French colony of Dominica. Out of the total population of the Caribbean, only 0.18 per cent are Carib Indians. They are among the least-reached, the poorest and most deprived peoples in that part of the world – and that in a region where Christianity is on the whole vibrant, with 70 per cent of the population perceived as 'Christian'.

No wonder the Carib Indians have found it difficult to embrace the gospel, no wonder they have clung on to their tribal animist practices. They mistrust white Christian Europeans because of the crimes perpetrated against their forefathers; they mistrust black Afro-Caribbean Christians because they were settled in their traditional homelands.

We have blood on our hands!

The passing of William Wilberforce's Bill for the Abolition of Slavery in 1833 would, one would have thought, have heralded the end of the scourge of slavery. It was sadly not the case. With the supply of slave labour from Africa cut off, attempts were made to exploit the Act and introduce an apprenticeship system. Former slaves were forced to work **unpaid** for forty and a half hours a week for their old masters for a period of seven years! This of course was the source of extreme unrest among the slaves, to which the sugar-plantation owners used brutal measures to retaliate. Eventually the system broke down completely – the owners were unwilling to pay wages to the now free Africans, who left the estates. With another source of labour urgently needed for the sugar plantations the men-merchants had to look elsewhere. They needed to find a way around the law. The British slave-masters went to India and the Dutch to Indonesia.

It was the era of the colonisation of India. The British treated the Indians in the same way as they had treated indigenous peoples all around the world. They regarded them as inferior, as less than human, as a resource to be exploited, as a race to be subdued. Women and children were sometimes abused and used in government-run houses for prostitution. Men were forced into slave labour.

At the same time, Christian missionaries from Britain came to convert the Indian people from their false religious ways. Christianity was regarded by the Indians as a European religion, not an Indian one. Christian missionaries tended only to go to certain places – where the hills made the climate more conducive – with the result that only those places became Christianized.

One Asian leader commented to me: 'You came and invaded us, destroying our religion. But now we recover and want to reverse what has happened. So we now come to convert you to Hinduism, Sikhism and Islam.' The biggest Hindu temple in the world has been constructed in London. 'You came as traders and took our wealth. So Europe is now receiving God's punishment.'

By subterfuge and empty promises of wealth, Indians were persuaded to become part of a force of 'indentured labour' who were shipped to the Caribbean. From 1838 to 1917 Indians suffered the same dehumanising processes which had characterised African slavery. Instead of a sea journey of four to six weeks from Africa, the voyage from Asia lasted three to four months. Many didn't make it. Up to a third died from cholera, typhoid, dysentery, and a dozen other diseases aboard ship.

Recruiters eventually took to kidnapping men and women to make up their quotas. The law stipulated that there should be a ratio of thirty-five women to every hundred men shipped to the West Indies. Most Indian women were betrothed as children and married at puberty, so those generally persuaded to go, or who were kidnapped, were either prostitutes, widows or girls who had left home.

The sexual imbalance put intolerable strain on relationships. Plantation owners and overseers formed relationships with Indian women. Unfaithful wives were sometimes murdered or beaten viciously. Sexuality became also a matter of trade. Today one of the major disgraces of West Indian society is the abuse of women:

> 'The modern tradition of wife-beating is one rooted in a shameful ancestral past of sexual competition on the plantation.' [2]

The indentured labour scheme promised workers a free return to their homeland at the end of five years. But in reality few were able to make that return. Between 1841 and

1851 over 42,300 Indians entered Guyana, but the population only increased by 29,500.[3] The rest died. In fact 30 per cent of those making the journey died en route – a total of 100,000 in seventy-six years – and 238,000 settled in Guyana. Beating and flogging of indentured labourers was a routine element in plantation discipline, right into the twentieth century. Up until 1870 those who reported sick were placed in stocks.

The atrocious conditions and the brutality provoked a backlash of riots which occurred with a sickening regularity. The peak was 1888, when forty-two disturbances were reported. Plantation hospitals were described by a Royal Commission as 'filthy holes'. Squalid accommodation remained unchanged throughout the seventy-nine years of the indenture period.

Philip Mohabir, a highly respected British Christian leader, was born in Guyana into such an 'indentured' family. His grandfather was persuaded by agents of the East India Company to leave his native India to go and 'pick up gold from the streets' in the West Indies. He was offered free passage, free food and a free return after five years – but he could return after six months if he wished, for he would make enough money from the gold to keep himself and his family for the rest of his life. Empty promises!

When his shipment arrived in the West Indies, the labourers were split up and sent all over the colony. Brothers and sisters were separated, and did not know where their siblings were taken. Parents and children were divided. They were treated just like the African slaves had been treated, and were made virtual prisoners of the sugar lords. They worked seventy to eighty hours a week for a pittance – a basket of basic groceries and a few pence. Few were able to return to India. Those who did manage to save enough money couldn't find their way back to their native villages or find their families. So, even in their homeland, they continued to be victims of the system of indentured labour.

Even fifty years ago African slaves were still kept in 'nigger pens', fed out of a common pot, and forced to sleep in appalling conditions with no sanitation. Children walking

along the street had to get into the gutter if a white man
came along.

I asked Philip Mohabir what a typical Asian felt like today.

'Asians have been scattered by the British around the
world. Taken as slaves to other nations, they still feel
slaves there now. Unable to leave, they feel alienated
from their own nation, and alienated in their adopted
one.'

In Guyana there remains the threat of violence between
the Afro-Caribbean urban minority and the East Indian
marginalised majority. In how many other situations does
modern-day ethnic rivalry and bitterness have at its root the
movement of masses of people for commercial or political
ends?

So our colonisation of other lands has been achieved in
two ways:

– by the subjugation or extermination of the indigenous
  population, or
– by the enforced movement of large numbers of people to
  a nation, culture and climate far away from their homeland.

The resulting anti-British and anti-Christian feeling is under-
standable.

What effect has the gospel had on those who have been
forcibly shipped to the West Indies? In Guyana, 70 per cent
are Hindu, 18 per cent are Muslim. In Surinam nearly all have
remained either Hindu or Muslim, and the Indian community has shown little response to the gospel. In Trinidad the
largest non-Christian element is among the East Indians.

Why is this so? It is surely because the slave traders and
sugar plantation owners were perceived as Christian. They
were from a Christian nation, they attended the Anglican
Church, their managers in England were influential in
Parliament.

'The establishment had the backing of the Anglican
Church. Outside some of the churches were notices
saying, "No dogs or black people".'   (Philip Mohabir)

Moravian missionaries who went to the West Indies to evangelise and teach on the plantations were eventually banned. Some were imprisoned, tortured and martyred – by the 'Christian' sugar lords – for working among the slaves! But it is probably largely due to the faithfulness of those Moravians that so many of the Afro-Caribbean population are Christian today.

The legacy of our colonisation of other parts of the world is similarly a mixed blessing. In parts of Africa there is profound gratitude for the positive good that Christian missions have brought through the gospel, in the form of health care, education and agriculture. We need to praise God for that. But at the same time we have to acknowledge that in those areas where the Church is weakest, where Christianity has made few advances, there are often historical reasons that point to the sin of the Church or the identification of the Church with the sin of our nation.

In India, for example, it is surely not surprising that the Church is weak and ineffective in those states from which the majority of indentured labourers were transported to colonise other lands? Why is it that in states and cities where Christianity is strong, there are still such acute moral and social problems? Bombay has the second highest Christian population of any major city in India (5 per cent), but has a reputation for vice, child prostitution and a frightening mushrooming of AIDS. In the state of Manipur nearly all the tribal people have become Protestant over the past eighty years, yet drug addiction and AIDS are major problems. We only have to look at the record of British occupation and its active encouragement of child and female prostitution to see a connection. Wherever the Church has countenanced sin, or been identified with its perpetrators, it gives licence for a continuation and increase of that sin in the population in succeeding generations.

The Indian subcontinent has suffered much at the hands of the British. The enforcement or proactive encouragement of migration for economic gain involved the move of Asian Indians to Kenya, Uganda, Malaysia and Indonesia, as well as to the West Indies. Even the enforced movement of Indian Tamils to Sri Lanka to engage in work among the tea plantations may be a factor in the recent civil unrest in Sri Lanka involving the Tamil Tigers. In every place these migrations have created a minority group in an alien society. Some of them have become trapped, without rights, and this has resulted in hostility by the host nation or tribes towards them. Even within India internal migration of tea workers to develop other tea estates caused similar problems.

As outlined in chapter 12 with reference to the Opium Trade, the duplicity and greed of the East India Company working out of Madras, Bombay and Calcutta was later built on by successive British governments. Again and again, the sins of the past have left a legacy in the present in size far greater than the former sins. And in the place where they initially took place a reputation builds that blights the people and the area.

The British Colonials also instituted a policy of 'divide and rule', which played off the Hindus against the Muslims, and which eventually led to the partition of India. In one sense British rule brought an end to 2500 years of division. India became one nation. But the policy of creating ethnic and class division and racial and economic imbalance always leads to unrest. So today we see the evidence in violent clashes between Hindu and Muslim separatists wherever one religious group is in the minority and views itself as being discriminated against. Internal tensions and clashes have steadily increased because of caste, religious and regional loyalties. How much of that is a legacy of the 'divide and rule' policy?

The educational system produced a nation of clerks who could serve in the civil service under the rule of the British. Even today 'entering Government service in any way, shape or form is the main expectation of high school matriculates'.[4]

But it is in its economic policies that Britain has shown its greed, its manipulation, its exploitation and its disregard for the ultimate well-being of the peoples it has plundered. Cecil Rhodes, architect of colonial rule in Africa, stated that the purpose of colonialism was:

'... to find new lands from which we can easily exploit the cheap slave labour that is available from the natives of the colonies; the colonies would also provide a dumping ground for surplus goods produced in our factories.'[5]

Two hundred years ago Dhaka was one of the major cities of the world with a population of 200,000. It was prosperous with a balanced economy and sufficient food, a thriving cottage industry, and an export trade in silk, cotton and jute. When the East India Company came along it exported jute and cotton from the region to prime the Industrial Revolution back home, and imported cheap manufactured goods made with child labour back into the region. This destabilised the cottage industries. Industrial machinery was not allowed to be exported from England, and because of high import taxes it was uneconomical to import silk and cotton produced goods. Within half a century Dhaka had 'fallen off from a flourishing town to a very poor and small one.'[6] At the time of partition not a single jute mill existed in East Pakistan, although the majority of the world's jute was grown there. This process became known as the 'famous Bengal plunder', because it helped to finance the Industrial Revolution in England and led to the ruin of the economy of Bengal.

Dr Steve Brown, a former TEAR Fund worker in Bangladesh, has commented: 'The whole purpose of colonialism was profit'. Whilst some may say 'Of course, the purpose of all business is profit', this necessarily disregards the well-being of the exploited. When our trade is deliberately aimed to make others poor and ourselves rich it is exploitive. When that is also seen to be linked with a Christian world-view, it is diabolical. 'Christianity, popularly known as the religion of imperial Britain, was closely interlinked with colonialism both in Asia and Africa.'[7]

Today for example, tobacco advertising has many restrictions placed on it in this country. Smoking is increasingly seen as a socially unacceptable practice and medically harmful. Yet in Third World countries cigarette advertising is blatant, exploitive and without any regard for the harmful effects it has on health. Commerce continues to make profit from the poorer classes and nations without regard for their health or economic well-being. Thankfully in the culture of today it is not so much seen as intertwined with the Christian gospel. But in the colonial period it was.

The third area of exploitation was in regard to land. In 1793 Britain, under Lord Cornwallis, introduced the Zamindari system, by which it created in Bengal a new class of landowners. Crown lands were dispensed to *zamindars* (local agents) who collected revenues and gave the Crown its appointed share. They were given proprietary rights in the land including sale and purchase, on the understanding they would procure large revenue returns for the Government. Village dwellers and agriculturists were made tenants, their hereditary rights ignored, and they became helpless and at the mercy of their landlords. Thus a system of feudal control was established. Those who failed to pay their taxes had their land confiscated. The result was that 'leech cities' and their zamindars sucked the life out of the countryside. Because of this land policy nearly one-third of the rural population of Bengal died of hunger and starvation in the 1770s during a massive famine!

Today Bangladesh is one of the poorest nations of the whole world. It feels inferior. Partition did not solve its problems. West Pakistan appears to have carried on a similar policy to make itself rich and its Eastern region poor. The eventual war for independence in 1971, fourteen years after Partition, did little to change things.

If a Bengali in Bangladesh is asked, 'What is a Christian?' the common answer is, 'Someone who drinks alcohol and is immoral', plus other phrases which are unmentionable in a book! Christianity is viewed as the religion of the oppressor. If we as British and as Christians are not moved by this legacy of antagonism to us and to our Lord, then what hope is there for the masses of the world's poor and religiously alienated peoples?

We have looked in brief at the West Indies, India and Bangladesh. But the same kind of issues emerge in almost every nation that we annexed in our British Empire. We could look at the blood shed in the massacre of Amritsar, at the battles fought with the tribes on the violent North West Frontier, the conflict and wars within India during the period of the British Raj. But we have shared just the tip of the iceberg – that which God in His wisdom has brought to our notice. How much more is there? We shall see.

Notes

1. Eric Williams in *Capitalism and Slavery*, cited by David Dabydeen in *Third World Impact*, edited by Arif Ali (Hansib Publishing, 1988), p. 123.
2. From *Features of Indo-Caribbean History* by David Dabydeen, cited in Arif Ali (ed.), *Third World Impact*, p. 125.
3. *Third World Impact*, p. 116.
4. Richard W. Timm, in a paper 'Perceptions of British Colonialism', August, 1995.
5. Cited by Richard W. Timm in *Power Relations in Rural Development* (Centre for Progress of Peoples, 1983).
6. Teresa Hayter, *The Creation of World Poverty* (Pluto Press, 1981).
7. D.A. Low in *Lion Rampant: Essays in the Study of British Imperialism* (F. Cass, 1973), p. 118.

Chapter 7

Britain and its Slaves

'The experience of African slavery and Indian indentured labour in the West Indies and its unjustifiable defence have, understandably, left a residue of bitterness in the minds of successive generations of West Indians. The West Indian struggle for political rights and economic justice, the movement to be rid of British colonialism and to establish independent states, were natural outgrowths from the anger aroused by these two brutal systems.'[1]

Stories of the slave trade from West Africa to the West Indies are well known. From the time of the Portuguese exploration of West Africa through to the colonisation of many parts of Africa, the trade in humans has flourished. Sadly, it still occurs today. What the white Europeans instigated in their colonial period, the Arabs continue in the modern world. There are stories of thousands of Sudanese being shipped by Arab slave-traders to other parts of Africa. 'The centuries-long slave trade was the greatest and most protracted genocide in history. It destroyed societies, generated the wealth that built up western industrial capitalism and exacted a price that can never be fully calculated'.[2]

Slavery is, of course, not just a European problem. There were slaves in the Roman period, when the Church was formed; the Phoenicians had their slaves in pre-Christian times; the Jews were slaves in Egypt, and they themselves had slaves (see for instance Leviticus 25:44–6)! For centuries, slaves have not only been owned by their masters, but have been sold by one group to another.

One can argue about whether there is any possible justification for slavery, about whether or not there is a need for it in some form, but these are not the issues which presently concern us. What we want to address in this chapter are the injustices and inhumanity associated with slavery, and the legacy that both as Christians and as Britons we have left in those nations from which we took slaves, and among those nations which are today largely made up of the descendants of slaves.

The abolition of the Slave Trade eventually became law in the Caribbean in 1834. Most know that this reform was introduced into the British parliament by William Wilberforce, a Christian man. That is something we need to thank God for. But alas, as we have already seen (see for example chapter 6), that was by no means the end of slavery – not even by the British.

Before the 1807 Act, Britain's slaving record was as appalling as that of any other nation. One of the Christians of that period who sought to champion the cause of the poor and the slave was David Livingstone who had a deep love for the Africans amongst whom he lived and for whom he gave his life. He saw the brutalities inflicted on Africans by Portuguese, Arab, British and Boer slave traders. 'He saw long lines of mistreated slave gangs and was surrounded by evidences of the slave-traders' heartless business in burned villages, abandoned slaves and dead bodies.'[3] His method of dealing with this evil was to encourage other forms of trade, so that the profitability of other avenues would seem to be more attractive to the traders (both African and European) than the profitability in human degradation. The problem was, however, the ceaseless demand from other parts of the world for cheap labour. Through his exploration of Africa, Livingstone unfortunately opened up other routes for the slave-traders to exploit – something he would never have intended.

For the most part, however, the trade in human misery persisted unchecked. The Gold Coast, Ghana and other parts of West Africa had been among the first target areas. Thousands were shipped to the West Indies following the commencement of the slave trade in the Elizabethan era. With African slaves being found in London as early as 1555, English involvement in this despicable trade was pioneered by John Hawkins, and it is clear that slaves were not only discriminated against because of their status as slaves, but also because of the colour of their skin. In 1596 Queen Elizabeth I issued orders for black people to be shipped abroad, because 'most of them are infidels having no understanding of Christ or His Gospel.'[4] So enforced repatriation became an issue four hundred years ago, partly because of colour. In the eighteenth century compulsory repatriation applied to 'the black poor', the common criminals and beggars. Many were forcibly taken to settle in Sierra Leone even though they had been granted their freedom in England. Once there they became prey yet again for the slave trade.

Racism is not a modern problem, nor exclusively a British one. Racism – the exploitation and devaluing of one person or group by another on the basis of colour, creed, language or race – has been with us for well over two thousand years. As we see from the Old Testament, God intended that different people groups should have distinctive racial identities. But we find that the Jews, the Philistines, the Babylonians, Amorites, Hittites, Jebusites, Moabites, and Canaanites were all either victims or perpetrators of racism at some time or other. The New Testament, however, talks about there being in Christ neither Jew nor Greek, neither male nor female, neither Scythian, barbarian, slave nor free (Colossians 3:11 and Galatians 3:28) – *'but Christ is all and in all.'* It is evident from this statement that Paul had to address the presence of racist attitudes in the early Church. With his statement *'Bear with each other and forgive whatever grievances you may have had'* (Colossians 3:13), he affirmed that in Christ there is a different approach. The trouble is that few Christians down the centuries have adopted it.

Racism was not invented by the British, but again we have been guilty of it corporately in the way we have treated others, even though we have apparently been operating out of a Christian-based value system. As a nation we have been perceived to be acting from a Christian motivation when in all probability that has basically not been the case at all! What is at issue is a **perspective** of racism which has actively been encouraged by the Church, because it has been seen to be emanating from a so-called Christian country. Is it possible to be 'racial' in attitude without being 'racist'? We believe so. Racialism acknowledges differences in groups and cultures without the element of superiority/inferiority being present.

But do we display racialist attitudes or racist ones? Do we treat others as equal or as inferior? Do we welcome people of other nationalities into our homes as readily as we do those of our own nation? Do we support discrimination against them in jobs, housing, or in their mistreatment by the police? These are not political questions, but biblical ones. If we are honest, most of us would have to admit that the seeds (or should we say the fruit) of racism are still in us. And if that is true of us as Christians, how much more are such attitudes present in society? How long have they been present? In what ways have they been corporately encouraged by Government and Church? Have they been influenced and affected by policies our forebears were party to, so that a repetitive legacy of inbred feelings of antagonism to the English by racial minority groups has emerged? Wherever we as Christians are partly or wholly responsible for the perpetuation of such attitudes, then corporate repentance is necessary.

In 1995 I was taking part in a Prayer and Reconciliation evening in a downtown Boston church in the USA. Three-quarters of the thousand people present were black Americans – descendants of slaves – the remainder were white. A white lady came forward to acknowledge her own and her family's racism in heartfelt repentance. With deep sobs she confessed to having been brought up to hate black people. Her father had been a member of the Ku Klux Klan and had participated in meetings to hang black people. Her tears wet the shoes of the respected black church leader, before whom she knelt to ask for forgiveness. A deep wail seemed to fill the building as similar confessions were made throughout the auditorium. As a white man I stood with her and confessed my own racism. I had been brought up in it as a Britisher living in Bermuda, and had suffered a terrible beating because of a friendship I had struck up with a West Indian girl – at the age of five! Tears flowed everywhere. Then a white pastor with a significant ministry in the area came forward and in stumbling words asked for prayer from the Black Christians. 'We envy you,' he said. 'Your churches are vibrant and lively. Ours aren't. Yours are growing. Ours aren't. You're involved in social action. We're not. We need you,' he cried out. 'We need your prayers, your encouragement, your fellowship. Please pray for us.'

With that almost every white person rushed forward and, amidst their sobs, prostrated themselves on the floor for prayer. It was a powerful and precious time. Something broke in the heavenlies. Something broke in the experience of all present. Black people and white people, normally used to shaking hands in a formal way and keeping each other at the proverbial arm's length, now hugged and hugged each other. I believe God broke through that night. That very evening two other gatherings were being held in downtown Boston and the same thing happened!

I heard later that subsequent to these events God's blessing of salvation was poured out. Beforehand, about ten people per month were being converted to Christ while afterwards upwards of a hundred a month were being saved!

The next day President Clinton was reported as having made a major speech, in which he said that white Americans needed to apologise to black Americans for their racism and the many ways in which blacks had been maltreated in the past. Most Americans would agree that the major problem they face nationally is racism. Events like the one described will help to change the situation – at least for those involved, and maybe also on a wider spiritual scale.

Such apologies also need to be given by Christians in Britain – both to their black fellow countrymen and women, and to the world. They also need to take place within the Body of Christ. They need to be given both as Christians and as Britishers. Within the Body of Christ we need to apologise for the way in which we have marginalised and not welcomed our brothers and sisters who have come from the Caribbean, Africa, Asia and Latin America. We need to apologise for the remarks, attitudes and actions we have been responsible for that have added to the problem of racial isolation and rejection. We need to seek forgiveness for our lack of concern, care and common courtesy towards so many from other parts of the world. We need to repent of deep-seated prejudices and coldness of heart which have created distance between us, and to work out how our unity in Christ can find practical expression in the days ahead.

Where these racist attitudes may have come from is not really important. What is important is to recognise that they have existed among us individually and corporately, and have been expressed with injustice and prejudice. We need to go on bended knee to ask for forgiveness in Christ's name for those times when our English forefathers were guilty of discrimination and diabolical treatment of their fellow human beings of other races. If we refuse, how can racism be expurgated from us? We believe God wants to use this nation as a blessing to other nations in a humble servant role, with respect for people of a different racial or cultural background. But how can we fulfil our destiny as a father to the nation-states we have helped to create, if we harbour or allow to fester any form of racism in our hearts and culture? How can we bless them if we allow this racism to exist as a continuing barrier to the openness of others to the gospel, when brought to them by a white person?

In the New Testament epistles, Paul was addressing issues of race as much as anything, when he wrote about unity. Denominational differences didn't arise then. The early Church was made up of people from a variety of backgrounds. The disciples had among them Romans, North Africans, Greeks, Jews – in fact the first converts were drawn from a variety of places, cultures and languages (see Acts 2:8–10)! Paul was concerned about racial unity in the Church. It is clear that in almost every place where the Church initially thrived, congregations were made up of people from many backgrounds, because cities like Corinth and Ephesus were cultural and trading centres. One of the problems he was addressing particularly was the Jews' sense of superiority because of their special relationship with God as a people group, which expressed itself in matters to do with religious practices.

Some ethnic differences are evident in Acts 6. The Grecian Jews complained that the Hebrew Jews were getting food, whereas they weren't (Acts 6:1). Paul used the terminology associated with slavery to show that Christ had set believers free (see Galatians 4:3, 8, 9, 24), and then affirmed, *'keep standing firm and do not be subject again to a yoke of slavery'* (Galatians 5:1). He asserted that God has taken away our natural hostilities to make us citizens together (Ephesians 2:16–19) and gave instruction about the way slaves should act towards their masters, and masters toward their slaves (Ephesians 6:5–9; Colossians 3:22–4:1).

To us, slavery and racism are closely aligned. Almost the whole of the Caribbean islands is populated by descendants of the slaves brought there from Africa and India. It is among those from the Caribbean that racism is most keenly felt today. Their forefathers were maltreated and devalued as slaves; they were kept economically poor; they were discriminated against and became victims of injustice in a thousand ways; they have grown up with a slave mentality. It is then no wonder that in the big cities to which they emigrated after the Second World War, through the proactive encouragement of the British Government, they became the victims of racial prejudice, abuse and mistreatment. Our churches didn't accept them, so they formed their own congregations and denominations. They were given menial jobs, for the very reason they were encouraged to migrate here was because Britain needed some form of cheap labour at home to compensate for the losses sustained in the Second World War and to assist in the recovery programme.

'From the 1950s with the political awakening and the fight for independence, there had been a lot of intrigue, back-room dealings, and behind-the-scenes political manipulation. Economically the squeeze was put on these islands because so much of what Britain had to sell was contracted to their former colonies. They were then in a position to call the shots in terms of prices for island goods, and also to call the shots in terms of prices for the machinery to market their raw materials' (Philip Mohabir).[5]

Should we then be surprised if we have our riots in Brixton, Toxteth, Bradford and anywhere else where a minority is forced into the ghetto and views itself as being the victim of discrimination by the people, police, and by Government?

Our forebears rarely showed any signs of Christian principles in the way that they dealt with slaves and people of different races.

In Africa it is much the same. As the colonial power we were in the ascendancy. Whilst we have handed over the reins of empire to independent States, nevertheless the seeds of empire are still to be seen in the racially motivated attitudes that are sometimes expressed.

We have many friends from African and Caribbean backgrounds. Some of them are well integrated and take their place with pride alongside Europeans. We have a very high regard for them – they are gifted, wise and a pleasure to know. Some, however, need a great deal of encouragement. They are gifted, have strong opinions and are to some extent trendsetters among their own people, but still find it difficult to integrate as equals alongside white British people and other Europeans. They are the modern victims of the racism and of the slave era which so oppressed their forebears, the stigma of which continues to some extent to affect them today. Some of these Christian leaders have themselves been treated abominably. They have been beaten up on our streets, arrested and questioned by police, rejected by employers – all in modern Britain! They have been taught to be suspicious of their white brothers, and their experience tells them they need to be. Criticism and fear of rejection reinforce their sense of alienation.

What can we do about it? Within this country, we can take every and any opportunity to apologise and ask forgiveness for our own personal marginalisation of black people, and that of white Christians generally. We need too to go to their churches and their homes, as well as invite them to our churches and our homes. We need to go to their churches without waiting for an invitation. Issuing an invitation in written form is the white way of doing things. Turning up, showing fellowship, interest and love is the black way of doing things. Every time one of us has gone to a West Indian congregation, unannounced and uninvited, we have been asked to bring greetings. The first time I did so, I apologised for the wrong attitudes we white Christians had had and for our lack of welcome to them. What healing took place in that meeting, and subsequently between Afro-Caribbean and English evangelicals! But it has taken ten to fifteen years for real progress to be made.

In 1989 a particularly vicious racially motivated riot took place in the Brixton area of London. Violence had suddenly flared up – buildings had been set on fire, shops had been looted, people had been injured and race relations were apparently in tatters. Ten days later local black-led churches organised a Saturday celebration to try and speak into the situation and express their unity in Christ. I went along; I wanted to be there, to show solidarity with my friends and Christian leaders who lived there. I was one of two white faces on the platform, although there were others in the congregation. We had a masterly, rousing call for unity and acceptance by black Christians of white. One speaker said some things a white person would never dare to say: 'When you came to Jesus, he turned your black heart of sin to white. When you get to heaven, you're going to get a white robe. The angels will be dressed in white. You'd better get ready to walk in white yourself.' It was a rallying call to fellowship with white Christians. I was glad I was there – and so were they. At times of tension and need we certainly need to be alongside them and supporting them – not patronisingly, but lovingly. When they hurt we hurt, when they rejoice, we rejoice – and vice versa.

Nowadays one of our Caribbean friends says, 'Not another reconciliation event – we need some action together!' – and he's right. To my shame I've recently realised that, although I have been many times to black-led churches and to the homes of my Caribbean friends, there are some who have never been to my home. So I need to go out of my way to correct the balance, and be over-the-top in insisting that they visit us. For some it will be a very big step to enter a white man's home, because they may never have done so before. Overcoming such barriers is a good step in the direction of dealing with the legacy of the past but it can only be symbolic. The roots of racism and the results of slavery go very deep. It may take a generation of apology, forgiveness and reconciliation before things will permanently change. But there are other reasons for persisting in this: God is glorified by His people being together in unity; and the enemy gets worried when he sees the increasing fruit. He will know that racism is one accusation that can't be levelled at the Church any more, and it will be one less reason for people groups to be kept alienated from the gospel of our Lord Jesus Christ.

Notes

1. Ron Sanders, quoted in Arif Ali (ed.), *Third World Impact* (Hansib Publishing, 1988).
2. Arif Ali (ed.), *Third World Impact*, p. 418.
3. Cecil Northcott, *Livingston in Africa*.
4. From an Elizabethan proclamation quoted in *Black Settlers in Britain 1555–1958* (Heinemann Educational Books Ltd, 1981).
5. Quoted from a personal conversation in September, 1995.

Chapter 8

The New World

I was travelling on a bus in Korea seated alongside the first Aborigine I can remember ever meeting. His name was Tim Edwards – a wonderful English name! He was pure aboriginal – a big burly man. I asked him about his people and the major problems they faced today. I asked how they felt about their history. He told me.

Australia is just over two hundred years old as a nation – although the native Aboriginals will rightly dispute that. Far better to say that it is two hundred years since white settlers came. But what sort of people were these first settlers and what did they bring with them?

Two hundred years ago food shortages, harsh penal laws and the general displacement of people during the early stages of the Industrial Revolution had led to a growing criminal population in England and posed an urgent problem for the government. Leading social reformers of the day assumed that the best way to eliminate crime was by removing criminals from society and so they were exported to penal colonies. Until its revolution in 1783 America was the favourite destination for these convicts. Subsequently Britain had to look for a new location and chose the land discovered by Captain Cook in 1768, which was viewed as unattractive for European settlement.

The first convoy of settlers to set out for the New World consisted of eleven ships, carrying 759 convicts (188 of them women) and 13 children of convicts, 211 marines and officers to guard the convicts, and 46 wives and children. They set sail from Portsmouth on 13 May 1787, landing at Botany Bay on 18 January 1788 – eight months later!

Botany Bay was not deemed a suitable location for a penal colony, so the convoy moved further north to Port Jackson (now known as Sydney). Here the first permanent settlement was established on 26 January 1788 – the date now celebrated annually as 'Australia Day'. So the very foundation of modern Australia can be traced back to its convicts.

Expelled alongside the convicted criminals – consisting of murderers and thieves as well as those convicted of petty crimes – were Irish rebels, prostitutes, and men who had stood alongside the Tolpuddle Martyrs, many of whom were Christians. Tradesmen and craftsmen, they had formed themselves into the first 'Trade Union' of workers to campaign for their rights, but because they were considered to be rebels against their managers they were expelled as 'criminals'.

Imagine what it must have been like for those prisoners: cooped up for weeks on end in pitiful conditions with meagre rations; forced to leave behind all they held dear to serve in penal colonies in an unknown new world. What would have gone through their minds during those long, dangerous, exacting weeks of travel? With their physical endurance being stretched to the limit there would have been plenty of time for them to dwell on their sense of rejection, to feed their feelings of anger and of hatred towards the establishment, to plan their acts of revenge; and what of the emotional turmoil for those who were innocent of the crimes for which they had been sentenced? How would they have survived?

When the convoy arrived at Port Jackson, the women and children were left on board ship, whilst the men prepared a campsite. Eight days later they were brought ashore.

'Within an hour of their landing a fierce storm lashed the camp and the 548 male convicts with many of the guards overtook the women in an orgy of debauchery and rape throughout the night that only can be described as horrific. Some commentators believe this action was a premeditated act as guards had requested the release of extra rum rations "to celebrate" the occasion.' [1]

The children born from this debauchery became known as currency kids. The unwanted by-products of forced sexual union both during the long nightmare voyage and later, they were either abandoned and left to fend for themselves or they were discarded into homes of convenience, from which in the years to come men on leave took a succession of de facto wives and children to tend their houses. This was the foundation of the Australian colony. The first generation offspring were products of crimes against women! In modern Australia the dubious legacy of being a descendant of a 'currency kid' lives on. (Later the term began to be applied to those who were first-generation born in Australia, as distinct from those who had 'settled' there.)

Lawlessness was a feature of the nation's early life. People were hanged for stealing a loaf of bread, but drunkenness, laziness, rape, prostitution and the manipulation of women were not viewed in such a serious light and so were not addressed as they should have been.

There were frequent rebellions, including one by Irish convicts, which was put down in 1804. Another uprising in 1808 became known as the 'rum rebellion'. Certain settlers were given grants of land and became the landowners. In an effort to enhance their income, they sought to control the price of rum which from the beginning had served as the colony's main internal means of exchange. Successive governors failed to impose other economic systems. So with rum the early means of exchange, drink became a key feature of the emerging nation.

The convicts, and reaction to them, became the major theme of early Australian history. By 1850, when the banishment policy was abolished, more than 162,000 had been sent. About one third of them were Irish, and 20 per cent were women. Many had been convicted of petty crimes and were poorly educated. Some were young teenagers and children – our own young banished as rejects. They became the underclass and to some extent their descendants still are.

An Australian woman we both recently met told us of her history. Her forebear had gone to Australia as a teenager on the first fleet. Prior to that he had been imprisoned on a rotting hulk in the River Thames from the age of fourteen. His crime was theft – 'Sir, I was sore distressed', he told the judge. But because he had nobody to speak for him, he was imprisoned. At the age of seventeen he was on one of the convict ships to Australia. His rejection and shame has been carried down through the generations of that woman's family.

Two years ago I received an air parcel from Australia. In it were two letters and a handkerchief. One of the letters came from a politician, descended from a convict family. His forebear had been banished to Australia as a lad of fifteen for the crime of stealing a handkerchief! This Christian man was asking us to pray to break the curse over his family in succeeding generations, and to receive his apology for the crime that had been committed. He added, 'I herewith return the handkerchief'!

The sense of abandonment deeply felt by this individual is widespread in Australian life, especially among young people. The perception of many Australians is that Britain has rejected them over and over again. They believe that Aussie volunteers in the world wars of this century were put into the most vulnerable front-line positions, with the result that their losses were proportionately higher than ours. They maintain that when we turned towards Europe for economic and trade reasons, we again abandoned them as a nation. Many of those who had emigrated at that time found themselves being made bankrupt because of the abrupt termination of trading links and the consequent destabilising of their economy.

Recently it has been revealed that Britain put young Australians into the nuclear test zone of the Woomera rocket range, and into the testing area for chemical weapons. Currently in southern Australia there is alarm at the number of people linked to these tests who have developed dreadful diseases. In addition there is the scandal of the so-called 'orphans' sent to Australia from Britain some fifty years ago, which has recently been investigated by a parliamentary delegation from the UK. All records of the origins of these young Britons had been destroyed and only now have some of them discovered that they were separated from brothers and sisters and other family members! These are the tragic stories of the repeated abandonment of our own young!

The Aboriginals

It will come as no surprise to us to discover that the banished, rejection-riddled British outcasts of the penal colonies should seek to dominate the native population of the New World, imposing their will on them and rejecting all that they stood for.

At the time of the penal settlements in New South Wales there were an estimated 300,000 Aboriginals throughout Australia, although some estimates are as high as one million. They were settled mainly on the coasts, were primitive, and used the surrounding land as their hunting domains. Initially the Aboriginals welcomed the Europeans as the spirits of their ancestors and during the first decade few major confrontations occurred between them and the British. The early policy of the British was to treat them kindly. Amazingly no survey had been conducted preparatory to the settlement and so, for the British, everything was totally new. The Aboriginals taught them some of the basic skills of survival – such as where to find water and how to hunt.

Their trust, however, was soon to be betrayed. Having found that the natives were friendly, the settlers began to interact with them. They drank to the King's health with rum and then celebrated. Most got drunk – extremely drunk! They offered alcohol to the natives. It was new and unknown to them and they accepted. Once they had made the leaders of the people drunk, the settlers raped their women and children, and then enslaved them. They stole their possessions and their land. They made treaties with them, but first they made them drunk so that they could have their own way and take what they wanted.

Benelong, an aboriginal leader, was captured by the Governor's men when he was twenty-five years old. He was shaved and cleaned, forced to wear stiff British clothes, and taken to dinner with the Governor as a curio or plaything. He was taught to speak English, to drink alcohol, to forget his own culture and to dress like a fop. He became the favourite novelty for Governor Phillip and the colony's soldiers and convicts, but at night he was shackled like a dog to the cottage the Governor built for him. Eventually, after making him drunk again, he was shipped to England to be paraded as a specimen Aborigine.

Phillip believed, in accordance with Darwin's evolutionary theory, that the Aboriginals were the missing link between stone-age human beings and 'fully evolved whites'. There was only a short step from this belief to a barbaric system of treatment of indigenous peoples. Considered less than human, they could be hunted and murdered, a crime for which people could not be tried for a number of years. Aboriginal communities began to be destroyed on a large scale and there were massacres at many of the scores of settlements scattered round the coast of Australia.

A trade developed to obtain and sell specimens for scientific research: some Aboriginals were killed for display, others for science. Thousands of aboriginal graves were raided, and bodies and bones were shipped back to England. An Oxford research study[2] has revealed that nearly 10,000 graves were desecrated in this way. Aboriginal massacres offered a source of supply for skulls. A New South Wales missionary described an incident in 1840:

'A large number were driven into the swamp and mounted police rode round and round and shot them indiscriminately, until they were all destroyed – men, women and children. Forty-five heads were collected and boiled down for the sake of 10 skulls.'[3]

The shipment of body parts was once described as the colony's 'new export industry'.

Tasmania, formerly known as Van Diemen's Land, was taken over by the English from the Dutch in 1803. Many Irish convicts, sent to the penal colonies because they were regarded as a political threat, were banished to Tasmania. As the settlers took control of the island, the aboriginal population was systematically wiped out – at least five thousand were murdered. In one incident a line of troops was formed across the whole of the island. As they marched forward they had orders to kill or capture every Aboriginal they could find.

We effectively committed genocide against their tribes in Tasmania, where random killings, a government-approved policy of incarceration, and active programmes of capture caused the indigenous population to be wiped out. Aboriginal women were tortured and made to be sex-slaves. Some settlers killed Aboriginals and used their bodies to feed their dogs. 'Symbolic of these atrocities was the story of Truganini. By the time she was seventeen she had been raped, had seen her mother stabbed, her uncle shot, her step-mother kidnapped, her sisters captured and her betrothed murdered.'[4] The *Australian Encyclopedia* lists and describes thirteen separate massacres of Aboriginals in Australia. Only recently a previously unknown massacre site has been unearthed. Our friend Tim Edwards tells us that there are hundreds of such sites in Australia.

In the past couple of years, white Australia has been going through another agony of soul and heart-searching over the 'stolen generation'. Between 1880 and 1960, tens of thousands of aboriginal infants were forcibly taken from their parents and brought up in the 'civilised' surroundings of orphanages, mission schools and foster homes. Records of their family origins were routinely destroyed. Many became servants or labourers for white families where they were often abused and forced to work without pay. Today these Aboriginals do not know where they belong. They fit into neither culture and are rejected by both. In May 1998 the whole nation of Australia had its first national 'Sorry Day', when books of apologies signed by 300,000 white Australians were presented to aboriginal leaders. The Prime Minister, John Howard, has expressed personal sorrow for historic injustices meted out to Aboriginals.

We in Britain need to do the same. We showed the way, commenced the policies and committed the atrocities.

The Legacy

In Australia, as in all the countries where British colonial domination was experienced, there was a failure to distinguish between culture and the undoubted pagan practices that went alongside it. The Aboriginals were forced to assimilate Western culture. At that time it was regarded as 'the Christian thing to do', for other cultures were seen as pagan, and therefore ungodly. In this way, the Aboriginals lost both their identity and their culture.

The Aboriginals became the underclass, and they remain so today. So degraded and put down have they been over countless years that they still find it hard to discover a sense of purpose and pride in their culture. Many feel shame and humiliation that as a people they have allowed so much to be lost.

The official colonial policy throughout the eighteenth century was to treat Aboriginals as 'equals', with the intention of converting them to Christianity and European civilisation. But looking back we can see that such a policy failed to value them as people, to value their culture, their rights, their needs, and their future. In fact we practised a form of 'protectionism' that maintained the British in their lifestyle. Commentators have said that moving from a policy of protection to one of punishment was typical of early colonial government.

Protectionism was practised by the British throughout the world in order to get our own way in relation to land, supplies, trade and natural resources. Once problems arose, or the indigenous populations found out they were being swindled, they began to turn against the British. In the worst cases mass slaughter was used in order to try and eliminate threats to British interest.

We believe the feelings of overwhelming rejection so many of the convict population carried with them into Australian life were turned destructively against what was seen as a weaker or inferior people. In human terms one way to cope with rejection is to find someone else to reject. We pass on to others what we have suffered. Victims become perpetrators. The downtrodden tread on others in order to gain some 'self-respect'. And so it has proven in relation to the Aboriginals.

'The real Australians have a history of "nationhood" that some believe goes back twenty thousand years! Whilst today white Australians have one of the highest standards of living in the world, the Aboriginal standard is one of the lowest. Trachoma – an inflammation leading to partial or total blindness – is endemic. In Western Australia 75 per cent of

Aborigines under the age of twenty-one are believed to display the symptoms of the disease. The Aboriginal population in the Kimberley region have the highest incidence of leprosy in the world of 107 per 100,000. In Victoria an Aboriginal is forty-five times more likely to go to prison than a white.'[5]

A policy of 'protectionism' was to some extent also pursued in Britain's dealings with the native New Zealand population, the Maoris. They too were disenfranchised, and made to feel inferior citizens in their own land. The Waitangi Treaty of 1840 allowed the British to settle in exchange for guarantees of Maori land and natural resources. But this in effect made the natives second-class citizens. Their subsequent cultural dislocation put them at a social disadvantage.

No wonder then that in 1995 the Queen apologised publicly in New Zealand for the way that the Maoris had been mistreated and betrayed during the colonial era. And the New Zealand Government paid $169 million to the Maori Trust, and returned 70,000 hectares of land, along with an official apology. This all happened after white Christians had first engaged in symbolic acts of repentance with Maoris.

White Australia too still bears the legacy of those first British settlers. A few years ago I visited Tasmania and found to my surprise that in Hobart families still refer to themselves as descendants of convicts – that is their claim to fame! It provides them with a dubious sense of identity and gives them a certain notoriety. These descendants still carry around the ignominy of their forebears, the curse of being a reject – and it is a curse, for it can give individuals a licence to behave in a certain way, as if nothing can change. Today many Australians are proud when they find out that they are direct descendants of 'first fleeters' or 'convicts'. Even the current Premier has discovered such a pedigree!

I visited an old penal colony – one of the historical treasures of modern Australia – a permanent, always-to-be-remembered symbol of their heritage. It was set in a beautiful location, in a quiet, storm-protected inlet. It was the sort of place we in England might have turned into a country park or luxury hotel. But the Australians had chosen to preserve these decaying buildings alongside a well-constructed exhibition centre as a perpetual reminder that their nation is descended from convict 'rejects'. This was the same place where a gunman murdered many tourists on a shooting rampage in 1996.

To this day drunkenness is the main problem among the Aboriginals and among white Australian males. In Habakkuk 2 we read:

> *'Woe to him who gets evil gain for his house*
> *To put his nest on high*
> *To be delivered from the hand of calamity!*
> *You have devised a shameful thing for your house*
> *By cutting off many peoples;*
> *So you are sinning against yourself...*
> *Woe to him who builds a city with bloodshed*
> *And founds a town with violence!...*
> *Woe to you who make your neighbours drink,*
> *Who mix in your venom even to make them drunk*
> *So as to look on their nakedness.*
> *You will be filled with disgrace rather than honour.*
> *Now you yourself drink and expose your own nakedness.'*
> (Habakkuk 2:9–10, 12, 15–16)

What an indictment on our history!

Because of the behaviour of the early settlers and their untrustworthy ways, the gospel that they preached – a hard, imposed, Protestant gospel – has not been truly accepted among native Australians until more recently. Early experience of Christianity insisted that everyone had to attend worship on a Sunday, and so British culture and lifestyle came to be seen as 'Christian'. The Aboriginals could not see the difference between the white man's beliefs and his practices. When the white man's gospel has brought them only pain, misery, humiliation, rejection, drunkenness, and loss of rights, how can they respond to a gospel of forgiveness, hope, love, and faith? Distrust of white Australia is linked with suspicion of the Christian gospel.

The Aboriginals suffered the same fate as many native

peoples all over the world. For that we are surely guilty. We cannot turn the clock back, so what can we do?

Hope for the Future

If we turn back to Habakkuk, we see two verses of hope. Chapter 2 starts with intercession. In chapter 1 Habakkuk has complained about the ways of the wicked. As he looks out on a world gone wrong, he asks:

'Why dost Thou make me see iniquity, and cause me to look on wickedness? ...
Why dost Thou look with favour on those who deal treacherously?' (Habakkuk 1:3, 13)

Then he waits for God's answer. It's not one he wants to hear. And quite honestly it's one I find terribly uncomfortable and heart-rending. From verse 2 of chapter 2 God pronounces His woes and His grief (verses 6, 9, 12, 15, 19) against nations in general, but against His people in particular. Woe after woe after woe. It's not what Habakkuk personally has done, but what God's people in the past have done. The world acts that way, God is in effect saying, because My people have acted in that way.

'You have looted many nations ... Because of human blood-shed and violence done to the land, to the town and all its inhabitants ... [twice he says that] ... you will be filled with disgrace.' (Habakkuk 2:8, 16)

And yet right in the midst of this comes that wonderful promise:

'For the earth will be filled with the knowledge of the glory of the Lord, as the waters cover the sea.' (Habakkuk 2:14)

We believe it is God's intention to deal with the sin of His people, to release them from the guilt of it and prepare the way for the earth to be filled with His glory. If that is so, then we must begin seriously and deliberately to acknowledge our terrible corporate sin as a Christian nation – firstly before God, and then before those we have so grossly offended, demeaned and sinned against. We need to apologise and beg for forgiveness. Only then will it be possible for the honesty of the gospel of God's love to flow out again. Only then can those with rejection in their history begin to feel acceptance. Only then will the Father's love, that so many have heard about, but have rarely seen in action, begin to be demonstrated.

As we have already mentioned, it has been said that our destiny as a British nation is to be a father to other nations – particularly to those nations like Australia, New Zealand, the Pacific colonies and to the more than forty other Commonwealth nations to which we have given birth. But even in our most recent history we have turned away from them for political and commercial reasons, seeking our trade and favour in Europe.

Our politicians may well argue that it is time for our offspring nations to stand on their own two feet, to take their place in the world in their own right. One can't argue with that. But can it be that we don't like our history, and we don't like feeling obligated by treaties and blood-stained ancient ties? So we react in a very human way and try to gloss over, forget, and cut ourselves off from our past wrongs.

This is, however, not the Christian response. The spread of the gospel is at stake here and so is righteousness in the nations. If we don't break the cycle of wrongdoing it will be repeated again and again in successive generations just as drunkenness has among Australian males. No, we need to face up to our continuing responsibility to our offspring nations – to be a father to them. What better way to start than by apologising for the terrible conception they had in the family of nations; to assure them of our desire for their spiritual, economic and social well-being, and of our willingness to do whatever is necessary to aid that process.

To some extent Queen Elizabeth II's attempt to maintain the Commonwealth of Nations is an expression of this. Having said that, those nations who participate sometimes do so, it seems, with mild tolerance rather than with wholehearted commitment to a common vision. A bit like the British themselves!

But what can the Church do? Our main motivation has been in the spread of the gospel. But for the gospel to be effective, its messengers have to have a lifestyle consistent with their message, and be willing to follow the message through with visible demonstrations of God's love. Can that happen for the Aboriginals? And for other Australians? Today Australia is as international as Britain. If the sins of the past, that were taken from this country when other nations were settled, can be acknowledged by the people of God in Britain, then maybe the door will be opened for God's love to go into one ethnic group after another.

On our last day together in Korea, I sought out the aboriginal delegation. I wanted a photograph of them, to assure them of my prayers, to thank them for their fellowship and for sharing their hearts. I told them of my willingness to come to Australia anytime to help the healing and reconciliation process continue! I felt such love for them as we hugged one another. Rather tragically one of them said to me, 'You know, we still don't feel really accepted by our white brothers and sisters. We still feel treated as second-class, inferior Christians.'

Why is that? Maybe it is because they have had so much rejection in the past that it will take a lot of reassurance for them to feel and be accepted as true equals in the Body of Christ. Maybe their white brothers and sisters haven't realised how much they need to go out of their way to include them in. There are such depths of sorrow, such humiliation, such anguish, that it will take a lot of love to break through. Change can only come when we face the fruits of racism and passed-down attitudes, recognising how much the past has shaped our own lives, and seek God's grace to deal with it. There is an abundance of God's grace available for all of us.

Notes

1.   Jim Nightingale, Brisbane House of Prayer (Quarterly Bulletin).
2.   Quoted from an article (without original source) in *Daily Telegraph*, 26 April 1994.
3.   Ibid.
4.   *Australian Encyclopedia* (Australian Geographic, 1996), p. 106.
5.   From 'World Minorities and Justice', in *Third World Impact* (Hansib Publishing, 1988), p. 127.

Chapter 9

Treaties and Treachery

The French call the English nation 'La Perfide Albion'. According to the *Readers' Digest Oxford English Dictionary* definition this refers to 'alleged treachery to other nations'. *Perfide* means treachery; *Albion* is an old Celtic word applying to England. Whether we speak of treachery – a violation of faith or trust – or traitors – those who commit acts of treachery – the implication is the same. As a nation, in the eyes of some, we have the reputation of not being trust-worthy, of betraying people, of breaking our promises.

At the human and personal level we all have a tendency to break our promises from time to time. We promise to meet someone at a certain time and place, but fail to turn up. We promise to write a letter, or make a phone call, but never do it. We fail to fulfil others' expectations. Jesus condemned such casual behaviour when he told the story of the man who promised to go to work in his father's vineyard but failed to turn up, and his brother who refused to go at first, but then relented (Matthew 21:28–32).

Breaking promises can be seen as a by-product of sin. God is the only One who has never broken a promise. In fact God cannot break promises – it is against His character. Not one of His promises has ever failed (Joshua 21:45). On the contrary, His promises are very great and precious – they are so special because they are unbreakable!

We, on the other hand, tend to take promises lightly: the promises made in marriage or in business are entered into so casually that for some they are hardly worth the paper they are written on. Couples today are even encouraged to enter into marriage with the full intention that if it doesn't work out they can go through a divorce.

In England, when legally binding promises or contracts are broken, the offenders can be taken to court. When travel agents fail to fulfil what their brochures promise, disenchanted holidaymakers sue for damages. When builders use shoddy materials or inferior workmanship, they can be prosecuted.

When as a nation we enter into similar sorts of contracts to protect a nation's borders, or to supply goods or services, we are acting in the same way corporately as we do individually. We have an obligation to keep our promises. As a so-called Christian nation, it is even more important that when we enter into such promises or treaties, we must abide by them, however inconvenient they happen to be at the time. Promises made internationally should be kept. Our reputation as a nation requires it. Our commitment to the Christian ethic and belief demands it. Failure to deliver makes us untrustworthy.

If such an attitude characterised our business dealings with overseas customers, as well as our governmental contracts, we would be a nation that could be trusted. We would worthily reflect the character of God. If we cannot do this, then maybe a clear distinction needs to be drawn between Church and State.

Successive governments have pursued foreign policy on the basis of what is in our best interests as a nation. Some may wish to dispute and debate whether this is a valid foundational principle for a government, but like it or not, it is the policy by which decisions are taken. At the very least, one would have thought, we would keep to what we have decided is 'in our best interests'.

Having said that, we ought to add that when we enter into alliances, allegiances and agreements, it is in order to pursue the nation's best interests 'at the time'. For if circumstances change, if a government changes – theirs or ours – or if policies change, then it seems we feel free as a nation to change our mind. We are like the British weather – changeable! We are apparently more influenced by an existential philosophy – whatever seems right at the time – than by the well-being and interests of others. We vacillate so much, with the result that around the world we have come to be perceived as a dishonourable nation.

The Munich Declaration

A couple of years ago while attending a small Europe-wide consultation of prayer leaders, a Czech leader spoke to me about his people's mistrust of the British as a result of the Munich agreement. When I later travelled to Prague for a conference for Christian leaders on 'Reconciliation of the Nations', I went prepared. Representatives from most of the Central European nations were present. These nations had experienced much animosity and ethnic hatred, and because of these historic antagonisms, some delegations weren't even on speaking terms with each other. We had come together particularly to pray over the former Yugo-slavia – that land racked by ethnic strife between Serbs, Croats, Hungarians, Bosnians and Albanians.

There was plenty to pray about. The first two days were spent confessing the sins that divided nation from nation and ethnic group from ethnic group, and asking for forgive-ness from one another.

In the first session of the conference, a Czech leader expressed his concern over the historical sin of Britain's betrayal of the Czech and Slovak Republics (and other nations) through the Munich agreement. A few months before the outbreak of the Second World War, Britain had signed an agreement to protect the borders of these nations from invasion by Hitler and if necessary to come to their aid. However, when Hitler did in fact invade in the early months of the war, no help was forthcoming. The British Govern-ment apparently thought that by sacrificing Czechoslovakia we could save our own nation from invasion and prevent a wider conflict. What a forlorn hope! The sacrifice of Czecho-slovakia was greeted with joy by the British public because it appeared that war was being averted. All we were interested in was ourselves. Our policy of self-interest was in operation yet again.

As a consequence of our policy of appeasement, our

blatant duplicity and disregard of allies, tens of thousands of Czechs and Slovaks were killed, Jews were hauled off to certain death in the concentration camps, Christians were imprisoned, churches requisitioned, and the whole nation of Czechoslovakia became an occupied power for fifty years. Whatever the reasoning, our lack of action was interpreted as betrayal.

Czech and Slovak soldiers, trained and ready to fight the Germans at the outbreak of war, were instead conscripted by the Germans to fight for them against the Russians. At the end of the war, now allied to Russia, soldiers who survived found themselves in the Russian army. It is only since 1989 that they have had their freedom. No wonder they look at Britain and say, 'You have caused us to be enslaved for fifty years because you reneged on your agreement.' And when the archbishop of the day, Cosmo Lang, equated 'the expediency of the Munich Declaration with the will of God', the Church is seen again to be formally backing Government policy.

Issues like this are real, profound and heart-rending and indicate deep feelings of betrayal, rejection, hurt, mistrust and suspicion in the hearts of the Czech people. We cannot afford to ignore them.

Like them, we were supposed to be a Christian nation, although much of our Christianity was nominal. Like them, we were products of the Reformation. In fact it was a Czech, Jan Hus, who was one of the architects of the Reformation. We had a common Christian heritage – and yet we let them down.

I was deeply ashamed of being British. I was ashamed that we had ignored them in their hour of need. I was grief-stricken to realise how much suffering they had been subjected to. Churchill was convinced we should have acted sooner against Hitler – but a war-weary nation was not ready to listen to him. I wished we could have turned the clock back. So, as the shame of what we had done began to hit me at this Prague conference, I stood up with the four other delegates from Britain and on behalf of our nation, my voice breaking with emotion, asked for forgiveness from our Czech brothers and sisters.

How can the horror of such sin be overcome in such a small, symbolic and, some may say, superficial way? I don't know. But at least for those present it was a meaningful response. Perhaps it was a start of a longer-term process. Until and unless Christian leaders take initiative on these issues, we cannot expect anyone else to notice. But as we step out, begin to humble ourselves and ask for the cleansing power of Christ's blood to be applied, we do begin to see a diminishing of the effect of that sin in the sight of God. The watching, gruesome, grovelling, grotesque enemy, Satan, who feeds off the cumulative effects of unconfessed sin, also, we believe, has some of his power taken from him by such acts. And when we accept responsibility on behalf of the nation, we begin to diffuse the antagonisms and hostility, and instead create a climate of mutual acceptance and co-operation.

The Pangkor Treaty

'Have you heard of the Pangkor Treaty?' I was asked at the international conference in Korea in 1993 where God had begun to burden both of us so much about these issues.

'No, what is that?' I asked in my ignorance. In 1874 Britain entered into an agreement with Malaya, handing over to the Sultans of Malaysia the Malay population, which today makes up 52 per cent of the country's total of nearly twenty million. The Malays are all resident in Peninsular Malaysia, and are prominent in politics, the civil service, the armed forces and the police. They are also predominantly agrarian. The agreement was made in order to bring to an end internal strife between the Chinese and Malays and between the quarrelling kingdoms of Malaya, as well as to find a solution to the frequent raids being made on trading ships and traders. So Britain acted as diplomat and policeman in bringing about a resolution of the conflicts. To some extent, too, we were motivated by our trading interests and the need to maintain a safe and secure trading base and trading routes.

'The Malay chiefs held positions of traditional prestige and importance in an ancient scheme of ritual deference, dating from the Malacca sultanate of the fifteenth century.'[1] Their

power depended on wealth. Loyalty to chiefs was consider-
able. They were the only symbols of order in an otherwise
fluid situation.

When the British Government looked for a group capable
of ruling in a complex situation, they chose the Sultans of
Malaya – who happened to be Muslims! The other two main
groupings – the traders (who were a hotch-potch of humanity, motivated by self-interest) and the Chinese (who were
mainly of the peasant class, organised into gangs and under
the control of warlords) – were deemed incapable of bringing
order out of chaos. So in the Pangkor Treaty, the control of
Malaysia was handed over to the Malay Sultans.

Britain could not afford to impose its will from London
through troop placements – it had to rely on local diplomacy
through the Colonial Office. Britain's much-vaunted 'divide
and rule' policy had the effect of keeping a divided nation
divided still, but controlled by the majority group in the
population. The treaty merely recognised this fact in handing over power to the Sultans, who then sought to impose
their will under a strict Muslim constitution.

Under the 'Pangkor Engagement', as it was known, the
rulers in every State of Malaya were required to seek and act
on British advice in all matters except 'Malay religion and
custom'. The mere fact of isolating Islam from the State
government in this way, meant that the Sultans could do
what they wished with religion, without reference to their
British colonial masters. As it happened, money was
provided in the annual budgets to pay the salaries of 'kadi'
and exalted Islamic officials. Today, as a result of this policy,
it is not permitted to evangelise the Malay population, and
those who do so are imprisoned, deported or even put to
death. In other words, by our treaty, possibly entered into
to promote British interests at that stage, we have effectively
isolated a whole people group from the gospel of Christ. For
over a century hardly any Malays have become Christians. If
they have, they have faced grave danger.

A significant Christian leader in Malaysia urged us recently
to do something about this treaty. As a direct result of it he
and his family were under threat of imprisonment and, in his

view, most of the persecution faced by the Church there can be traced back to it.

When we looked more closely at the circumstances surrounding the signing of the Pangkor Treaty, it had all the familiar ingredients of English self-interest. The East India Company had taken over both Dutch and French business interests. The 'Straits', as the area of Peninsular Malaysia and Singapore used to be known, was a very important trading station. China tea came through the area in return for Indian opium (see chapter 12). Convicts from India had been shipped to the area and became the cheap labour for the region. Planters and miners arrived from China in large numbers, having been displaced by the poverty created by the opium trade. So there was a strong potential for ethnic unrest. Anti-British feeling, particularly from the Chinese, continues to this day.

Trade became the number one earner for the area. Britain, as the world's leading trading power, knew how to exploit commerce, ethnic problems, slave labour and natural resources to its best advantage. In 1857 Britain took over control of the East India Company because of its apparent corruption. In 1858 a dispute arose concerning India's 'neglect and restraints in the region'. The matter was referred to the Government in London. After consultations between various departments spanning several years, the Colonial Office assumed responsibility for the Straits settlement by Act of Parliament in 1867, because 'it had long experience in many parts of the world in setting up administrations designed for specific needs'.[2]

The first Governor appointed was unpopular from the start. The powerful businessmen and traders in the region bombarded the Colonial Office with complaints about his administration. He was introducing all the elements of control, whereas they were lobbying for help in securing their trading interests. He managed to offend almost every-one who was of any importance in the colony. But given the circumstances he inherited, he appeared to be in a no-win situation. In London's view the colony was in the hands of mavericks operating to their own interests who needed to be controlled. Yet Governors were instructed to do all they

could to promote British commerce, without initiating political moves which might require armed intervention. London
was making every effort to keep trade and politics separate,
yet despite this the needs and demands of the traders were
often in conflict with those of the Malay chiefs or sultans.

In addition there was the problem of river and coastal
piracy – from both Malay and Chinese sources – which was
severely hampering commerce. Malay and Chinese authorities were viewed as unscrupulous and their areas as seething
with crime. Independent observers reported that the Straits
government had no policy or consistency of aim and
drifted from crisis to crisis. But the Malay rulers would
welcome treaties that would expand trade and provide
higher revenues for themselves.

So here were the seeds – different to some degree from
other colonies, but similar in character: seeds of British
arrogance and pride in considering they knew best how to
govern and rule; seeds of self-interest as British trading
concerns were promoted, no matter what the reactions of
the indigenous community, with wealth and prosperity for
Britain the prime motive for its policies.

The Malay chiefs wielded much power among the people.
Their prestige and power were linked to their wealth and
were exercised with feudal loyalty. The hold of religion –
Islam in most of Malay society – was more ceremonial and
spiritual than social. When left to themselves, the Malay
states were described as 'endemically unstable'. Another
source of power came from the influx of Chinese labourers
over many decades. Mostly poor and destitute when they
arrived, they worked hard under their British overlords, and
grew wealthy, and their wealth gave them equal status to the
Malay chiefs. They gained in strength and eventually were
able even to 'lend money to the improvident Malays, as the
Europeans did'.[3] Up country the Chinese overlords also
became petty warlords, able to defy Malay chiefs.

The British sought to provide the missing ingredient in all
this: law and order. A second Governor, Sir Andrew Clarke,
was appointed to implement this new policy but he went
further than the Colonial Office wished, and without
consulting them. Although he was initially given orders to

discover what the situation was really like, within two months of arriving he initiated the so-called Pangkor Engagement, which was signed in January 1874. Its effect was to require the Chinese population to disarm, to cease piracy and to be subject to Abdullah, the Sultan of Perak. It also resulted in the coming together of the sultans, or chiefs of the Malay States, under a British agent's rule for each of them. This hastily compiled treaty was to result in the Chinese being treated as second-class citizens from that time on, and kept power and rule firmly in the hands of the sultans. The fact that they were also Muslims reinforced Islam as the religion of the Malays.

So the Pangkor Treaty has been interpreted as being entered into to preserve British interests at the time, and therefore of consigning a whole people group to Islam.

Under the stipulations of her treaties with the Malay States, Britain became responsible for acting to stop disorder in the region. Other European nations were required to keep out. This is the reason for British involvement in the Malaysian War of Independence in the 1950s and 1960s. Because we have been seen as the ultimate controlling power throughout our colonial period, whatever may have been the rights or wrongs of the treaty, however questionable may have been the motives for it, the net result has been continued antagonism. We imposed a political solution, which ignored the rights of self-determination, and which actually pampered to the demands of a few influential and selfishly motivated individuals.

What of the ethics of breaking treaties? We seem to have had no qualms about doing so where it suited us. No doubt if the Pangkor Treaty were formally and publicly broken by the Government it would be acutely embarrassing in terms of our relationship with a fellow-Commonwealth ally.

With many treaties and Acts of Parliament the long-term repercussions are not always evident. The need for them ceases with time. Changes in lifestyle, language, political boundaries and behaviour make it important to review legislation from time to time. So Acts have been and are still being rescinded. A recent example is Sunday Trading legislation which has been abolished, allowing for a free-for-all.

That has been brought about by sustained lobbying by commercial interest groups. Can the Church learn from this? Can we not lobby our Government for the repeal of Acts that dishonour God, and the cancellation of treaties that served their purpose in the past, but which are an embarrassment to us today?

The maintenance of the Pangkor Treaty may be seen as a contravention of the United Nations Agreement on Freedom of Religion. The Malaysian Government's guarantee of religious freedom is being ignored by them. Could the key to this situation be for the Church and our Government to regularise matters by a repeal or amendment of that Treaty?

Illegal Treaties

Some of our treaties have been entered into illegally. We have obtained land rights by coercion, by conquest, and by fraudulent means. The Australian experience (see chapter 8) illustrates how we gained superiority through the use of alcohol. We've done that elsewhere in the world too: in India, the West Indies, North America – in fact, wherever our colonial power was expressed.

We have been guilty of corruption – giving back-handers in order to secure agreements to our advantage, or receiving bribes in order to line our own pockets. Businesses or individuals acting in this way today would be the subject of sleaze investigations, corruption trials, sackings from Government and national scandal. But because these trans-actions have been done on behalf of, and out of the sight of, national Government elsewhere in the world at various times in history, they go unpunished, and there is no account-ability. It is the same with illegally negotiated treaties: if they seem to be in our interest, their legality is not challenged. Is it not time for change?

In parts of North America settlers from these shores made native American Indians drunk in order to usurp the author-ity of their leaders and force them to enter into treaties to hand over their land. If the Indians refused to agree to their terms, they resorted to the physical option of forcibly removing them, or worse still, torching their wigwams and slaughtering their women and children.

John Dawson has written:

> 'Real reconciliation involves taking upon ourselves both the guilt and grandeur of our history and facing the implications squarely.'[4]

In recent years many white North American Christians have been going to the sites of massacres and illegal treaties, and before native American leaders have been repenting of the sins of the past and asking for forgiveness. Some in positions of responsibility in government or with influence in business, have been offering to recompense the descendants in practical ways.

One oil man, a deeply committed Christian, owned the natural gas rights to some land in the State of Wyoming. 'I pay royalties to the government on every well, but I am prepared to volunteer an additional royalty to the descendants of the Indians displaced from this area,' he said.[5] That is real repentance. That is more than mere confession and acknowledgement of guilt. He was prepared to do something about the sin, even though it was not his personally. Even though it was over two hundred years old. He recognised that as a Christian and as an American who was benefiting from the sins of his forefathers, he had to **do** something.

We need to do the same.

Isaiah 24 records God's anguish over the earth:

> 'The earth mourns and withers, the world fades and withers, the exalted of the people of the earth fade away. The earth is also polluted by its inhabitants, for they transgressed laws, violated statutes, broke the everlasting covenant.'
>
> (Isaiah 24:4–6)

Then the mood changes:

> 'From the ends of the earth we hear songs, "Glory to the Righteous One", but I say, "Woe to me! Woe to me! Alas for me! The treacherous deal treacherously, and the treacherous deal very treacherously." Terror and pit and snare confront

*you, O inhabitant of the earth ... For its transgression is
heavy upon it, and it will fall, never to rise again.'*

(Isaiah 24:16–17, 20)

Heavy upon us are the acts of betrayal and treachery we
have entered into. Heavy upon us are the agreements
we have illegally initiated and enshrined in law, that have
left a legacy of hate, fear, injustice and moral corruption.
Heavy upon us is our guilt. And heavy upon us must be our
resolve to confess in nation after nation our corporate sin.

We need to start on many fronts:

1. Intercessors need to research, with the help of *Operation
    World*[6] and historians, the areas of the world where our
    guilt has marginalised peoples, banished them to
    poverty, imposed unjust laws and so on. Then we should
    pray through these issues, seeking God for appropriate
    prophetic acts, opportunities for reconciliation, and
    means of restitution.

2. The Government may need to set up a Committee of
    Enquiry into past illegal treaties. Questions need to be
    asked about the nature of illegalities, how treaties were
    enacted, what the legacy of injustice has been and what
    restitution would be acceptable and appropriate.

3. Christian leaders need to take every opportunity to
    discover from the leaders of countries they visit or host
    in what ways we as British people have offended their
    people, and then to enter into meaningful acts of
    confession, repentance and reconciliation.

4. And for all of us, what about starting among the peoples
    from those nations who are resident in our own land?
    Let's find out from them how they view us, and then
    respond in a way that admits wrong, seeks forgiveness
    and builds positive relationship.

The years 1994 and 1995 gave the world a unique
opportunity to remember the end of the Second World War
both in Germany and in the Far East. The mayors of
Hiroshima and Nagasaki – the only two cities on planet earth
ever to be destroyed by atomic bombs – have apologised to

the world for the atrocities committed by the Japanese in the Second World War! They have appealed that atomic bombs should never be used again anywhere in the world. There have been calls by war veterans from the West for restitution from Japan for those who were scarred during the war, lost their freedom, their lives, their sanity, their limbs. At the end of wars there is usually a call for restitution and help in rebuilding the shattered lives of the dispossessed.

Has there ever been any restitution for our unrighteous acts committed in peacetime? Any acknowledgement of guilt? Any apology? Any sharing of anguish before God? Now is the time for *Perfide Albion* to humble herself and seek forgiveness.

Notes

1. Robert Heussler, *British Rule in Malaya (1867–1942)* (Greenwood Publishing Group, 1981), p. 7.
2. Ibid., p. 4.
3. Ibid., p. 8.
4. In *Healing America's Wounds* (Regal Books, 1994).
5. Ibid., p. 163.
6. Patrick Johnstone (OM Publishing, 1993).

Chapter 10

Munich and the Second World War

John Pressdee

The complexities and reasons why countries go to war is a subject too vast for us to study in these next pages. Whether it is because of greed, economic reasons, expansionism, or just power lust, the resulting suffering and slaughter mean that no nation wins. In the long term the people are the losers. However, there is no doubt that Germany were the aggressors in 1939 and there is no doubt that Hitler was a practising occultist who was driven by demonic forces. Having lived and worked in Germany for two and a half years, it is astonishing to reflect that such a charming people could entrust their collective consciences to a gang of ruthless thugs. The fate of the German nation was sealed when it embarked on its programme of ethnic cleansing in what was to be called 'The Final Solution'. Winston Churchill's words, 'They have sown to the wind, they will reap the whirlwind' (quoting Hosea 8:7), were literally fulfilled in the firestorm raids on cities such as Hamburg and Dresden.

It would be true to say that the reasons for Britain going to war in 1939 were more clear cut and the issues more black and white than in 1914 when the roots of war were pride and nationalism. It was in the trenches of the First World War that the Marxist dream of 'Working Class Solidarity' died and nations realised that only the nationalism that started the war could finish it. Here indeed the roots of Fascism began.

There is little doubt that the only option open to us in 1939 (apart from the whole nation repenting, turning to God and, like the Children of Israel in the days of the Exodus, trusting God to intervene supernaturally) was to go to war. When we reflect on some of the events of the last war and our involvement in them, it becomes a salutary reminder of the excesses and downright sinfulness that even the best of democracies are prone to stoop to under the pressures of war. As a nation, we are not guiltless in this matter.

If we were honest about ourselves and looked beneath the veneer of our British reserve, we might admit that we tend to view ourselves as a cultured, tolerant race of people who only get angry when faced by aggressors and bullies. Under extreme provocation, we might further concede, we react with a God-given sense of anger and mission, and against all the odds, we overcome, whether it be Drake against the Armada, Henry V at Agincourt or Dowding and the Battle of Britain. 'We few, we faithful few . . . '. Churchill used this facet of our national character to the full in his famous speeches. It is of interest to note that one of the fastest growing industries in this country is devoted to nostalgia and memorabilia and perpetuates our romantic, cosy view of history.

I remember the sense of shock and indignation I felt at a meeting in Lille, Northern France, as part of our prayer expedition from London to Berlin when my cosy view of history was shattered. We were discussing with a group of French pastors the possibility of a prayer celebration in Dunkerque, when one of the pastors said in no uncertain terms: 'Dunkerque is still a very painful memory for us. That was the place where you British ran away and left us.' It was a totally different view of an event that, although disastrous, we somehow contrive to hail as a triumph. As we talked more we began to discover that after fifty years people in France were still damaged by the events of the War and that reconciliation was necessary between us all – English and French as well as French and German. Delving deeper I learnt that events like the sinking of the French fleet in North Africa in 1940 by the Royal Navy had left the French – at least those I met – with bitter memories and that following the Normandy landings in 1944 they were more angry with the British than they were with the Germans! The devastating impact of British action was experienced in Normandy with the bombing of Caen by Bomber Command. One reliable report documented that the massive raid, which devastated the whole of the city of Caen, killed only three Germans, but five thousand French people died as a result. Destruction of a similar magnitude occurred at places like Lisieux where something like 98 per cent of the city was destroyed.

The emerging truth about Dunkerque was that we only managed to escape with our troops because the French and Belgian armies held the Germans off at Lille and other places. An astonishing fact of the evacuation is that we didn't even bother to tell the French Government that we were going: we just left the French to get on with it. It was only under pressure from the French Premier Reynaud that in the end we evacuated 30,000 French soldiers.

As we prayed through France alongside French Christians it became clear that the past had not been dealt with adequately and such events and memories still rankle and need to be healed. There is a lot of pride in us as English people and we tend to look down on other nations without realising that our own history at times leaves much to be desired. In 1995 I led a team of English, French and German young men and women walking from Berlin to Paris. It was a Jubilee prayer expedition to mark the fiftieth anniversary of the end of the War. As we walked and prayed together, we found ourselves repenting deeply in places like Vimy Ridge, the Somme battlefields and Flanders. Our hearts melted towards one another and we forgot our nationalities and became truly one in the Holy Spirit. That same French pastor who spoke of Dunkerque felt led to say of our prayer expedition, 'Our grandfathers and fathers fought against one another in two World Wars. We as their descendants walk together in love in the gospel proving that the power of God is greater than pride and nationalism!'

I have an aversion to revisionist historians who set about debunking our heroes and demystifying our heroic legends. However, one good reason for looking back on history is that we can see at times how badly world leaders performed and just how bravely they were saved and supported by their suffering and wonderful populations. Winston Churchill holds a unique mythological place in modern British history.

With the vast range of archival material now available to us over the last thirty years or so, a different picture of the statesman emerges. In it we see a man who 'wanted to forcibly sterilise over 100,000 mentally degenerate Britons, to send tens of thousands of others to forced labour camps, a racist who disliked democracy, who didn't believe in social progress and preferred rule by a small aristocratic elite. A man widely disliked and distrusted by his political colleagues for his egotism, overwhelming ambition and inconsistency.'[1] We now know for instance, that Churchill's fiery speeches that did so much to win popular support in America were in fact imitated by a BBC repertory actor called Norman Shelley, who with Churchill's permission, recorded all of his speeches for the Americans. Delusion is a most powerful thing.

If we go back to 1938, we see a shameful event that still has repercussions today. The event we have called 'The Munich Pact' elicits memories of Neville Chamberlain with his little piece of paper waving in the air at Croydon Airport and his now famous phrase, 'This is peace in our time.' We know in retrospect that, although a sincere well-meaning man, Chamberlain was duped by the Fascist dictators Hitler and Mussolini. Hitler's claim to Czechoslovakia's Sudetenland was based upon fictitious stories that the German people living there were being badly treated by the Czech government. It was not true, but the German press controlled by Goebbels' propaganda department told the story the way he wanted it to be told. In September 1938, Hitler, Chamberlain, Mussolini and Premier Daladier met in Munich to discuss Hitler's claims. With the Munich Pact signed, Chamberlain came back waving the agreement in triumph, an agreement that also renounced going to war.

This pact gave Hitler carte-blanche to grab the Czech border regions and by doing so he put the rest of the country in a very vulnerable position. The Czechs were given no say about the carving up of their country, but important to them and by way of consolation, Britain and France guaranteed the new frontiers against 'unprovoked aggression'. The whole meeting was a futile attempt to save our faces and pride.

Having occupied the Sudetenland, Hitler immediately began encouraging the Slovakians (a large section of the dismembered country) to demand freedom. Nazi demands on the Prague Government became more and more outrageous: 'Czechoslovakia must leave the League of Nations, reduce its army, turn over its gold to the Reichsbank, outlaw the Jews . . . ' etc. In March 1939, the Nazis, under the pretext of protecting Sudeten Germans, invaded the rest of the country. In London, the news that German troops had invaded and occupied Prague, contravening their previous agreement, came as a shock. Now was the time for the British to honour their commitment to the Czechs. Far from honouring our agreement, the Government, through Lord Halifax, the then Foreign Secretary, said, 'We haven't guaranteed the Czechs against the exercise of moral pressure, and in the circumstances, Britain's guarantee has ended.' Chamberlain not only concurred with this, but also blamed the Slovaks for wanting a separate state – 'That was what precipitated the crisis,' he said. At the time of the Munich Pact, Winston Churchill, a rebel backbench Member of Parliament said, 'We have sustained a total and unmitigated defeat, a disaster of the first magnitude.'

Our weak and sinful reaction and failure to honour our commitment to Czechoslovakia has left wounds of betrayal. Wounds do not go away even if scar tissue forms over them. Nearly sixty years on, the lessons and the pain of these events continue to reverberate and affect people's present-day judgements. In August 1996, as part of a walk of reconciliation from Cologne to Istanbul, we entered Prague and made an act of repentance towards our Czechoslovakian friends. We asked for forgiveness, for surely cowardice and betrayal are sins mentioned in the book of Revelation as reasons for being thrown into the Lake of Fire.

Dresden

When, in the latter stages of the war, Britain's power and prestige were being superseded by the greater military might of the Soviet Union and America, Prime Minister Churchill required a bargaining counter, or at least something to make him appear important and successful, for the forthcoming conference at Yalta with Stalin and Roosevelt. To achieve this, Churchill asked for air attacks on the civilian population in large cities rather than on military targets. His requests brought what was to be known as 'Operation Thunderclap' into operation. The official RAF history by Webster and Frankland states that the targets were to be 'Berlin, Leipzig, Dresden and associated cities where heavy attack will cause great confusion in civilian evacuation from the East and hamper movements of reinforcements from other fronts.' The British historians were honest enough to tell the whole truth that unfortunate, frozen, starving, civilian refugees were the first object of British attack, preferred before military objectives. Operation Thunderclap heralded a major increase in terror bombing. Its plan in essence in the latter stages of the war was to 'attack cities with populations of around 300,000 and inflict casualties of about 220,000 of which half would be deaths'. It was thought that 'such attacks ... cannot but have a shattering effect on political and civilian morale all over Germany.' Dresden, known as 'The Jewel of the Elbe', was a most beautiful city, famed for its architectural beauty and was of little strategic importance. Its very few military targets were ignored by the bombers whose aim was to destroy the city and to create an unstoppable firestorm. The target was the civilian population.

The attack produced a death toll of at least 100,000 people. The true number will never be known because so many refugees were in the city fleeing from the Russians and the firestorm with temperatures of over 3000°C left no human remains. People simply vanished. Weeks later, in an amazing about-turn, Churchill wrote a minute to the Chief of the Air Staff raising questions on the operation he helped initiate. 'The destruction of Dresden remains a serious query against the conduct of allied bombing.' Surely this is rank hypocrisy of the first order.

On 13 and 14 February, 1994, fifty years after the event, I led a team of British and German Christians to pray around Dresden. We were informed by local people that in the days following the raid, innocent people who had sought refuge from the flames in their local parks and by the River Elbe were mercilessly machine-gunned by allied fighters. Hind-sight is a wonderful thing, but surely this was an entirely horrifying and wicked event and can only be compared to mass murder. In a meeting of churches in Dresden on the evening of 13 February 1994, I stood with other British and American Christians and asked for forgiveness for this horrendous act. Our German friends responded magnificently. I believe that we have underestimated the desire of our German friends to seek repentance and reconciliation for their part in the Second World War.

There are many people today who still defend the Dresden massacre, mostly by pointing to German atrocities or by claiming it was a 'them or us' situation, all the while knowing that the city contained mainly women, children and old people. One author said:

> 'The final phase of Bomber Command's operations was far and away the worst. Traditional British chivalry and the use of minimum force in war was to become a mockery and the outrages perpetrated by the bombers will be remembered a thousand years hence.'

This does not make good reading. Some will argue that such raids hastened the end of the war and saved many other lives but this is an evasion of the issue. **Nothing** can justify such actions. Many of the men who were in such raids still to this day feel guilty, are haunted by terrible memories and wish they had never been involved.

One of these men in Bomber Command became a member of our team when we walked and prayed through Germany. He had flown many times over Germany and after the war, when he became a Christian, he began to feel very bad about his participation in the bombing of helpless civilians. He asked me if he could be part of our team and said that he wanted to be reconciled to German people, to ask for forgiveness and to be forgiven. All across Germany, in cities like Cologne, Dusseldorf, Hanover, Mac McCarthy would stand up in public meetings and ask for forgiveness and I personally witnessed hundreds and thousands of German people flocking forward to give him forgiveness and to ask the same of him. I remember one memorable occasion in Berlin, when in front of 60,000 people, at a March for Jesus rally, Mac stood up and said these words: 'I have been five times now to this city of Berlin, four times to bomb you, this time to ask for your forgiveness.' And I remember pastors kissing his feet and giving forgiveness. It is my deep conviction that on these occasions we were breaking down hostility in the heavenly places between our nations and making it possible for revival to flow between Great Britain and Germany. I personally believe that Paul Cain's prophecy of the supernatural link between Berlin and London was initiated by that event.

It's easy to be judgemental of our fathers as we look back with hindsight and perhaps it's true that one day we will have to say with Elijah, 'I am no better than my fathers' (1 Kings 19:4), but these are pains that still remain in Europe. However, the power of the blood of Jesus can reach back into the worst of our history – both personal and national – and as we go and repent, somehow we are making it possible for God to come in a way that has not been possible before because of our past actions and sins. As we have repented in Germany, France, Holland, Russia I have seen that God can heal us of past pain. In Russia, with a team of 400 people I witnessed Germans stand and ask publicly for forgiveness for the sins of their fathers, and I saw with my own eyes Russian people whose relatives had been murdered by the Nazis, publicly forgive them. The only answer for our society is the all-consuming power and love of our God.

I have not written to stand in judgement on our predecessors: we stood alone in 1940. If Germany had succeeded in invading us and then with only one front remaining, proceeded to fight on against the Soviet Union, the prospect of Axis forces joining together with Japan coming from the East would indeed have become a reality. One US general famously said, 'War is Hell' and this is true – we do not stand in judgement, but we will all have to stand in repentance before our God.[2]

Notes

1. Clive Ponting, *Churchill* (Sinclair Stevenson, 1995).
2. For further reading see: Clive Ponting, *Churchill* (Sinclair Stevenson, 1995); Alex McKee, *Dresden 1945* (Souvenir Press, 1982); Len Deighton, *Blood, Tears and Folly* (London: Pimlico, 1995).

Chapter 11

Britain and the Jews

According to a table of hate published by a national British newspaper several years ago, the most hated group of people across Europe today is the Jews. In eight of the ten countries polled, including seven from Eastern Europe and three from Western Europe (France, Germany and Spain), Jews were cited as one of the most hated groups, with an average of 20 per cent of the population saying they hated Jews. Hatred of the Jews is a worldwide problem – and an historic one. Ever since the children of Israel were given a special role in the purposes of God, nations have set themselves against them, and by doing so have been seen to set themselves against God.

Before we begin to consider the question of Britain's historical attitude to Jewish people and the Jewish nation we need to admit frankly that biblical Christians hold very different views about the role of the Jews as a nation in Christian theology. All agree on the key role of Israel preparatory to the first coming of Christ. The differences relate to its role since then, and its significance in relation to Christ's second coming. Basically it boils down to whether Old Testament prophecy about Israel was all fulfilled in Christ or whether some still remains to be fulfilled. Those who are strongly incarnational believe that all is fulfilled and it only remains for us to get the gospel to every tribe, tongue and nation (including the Jews) and then Jesus will return. Supporters of this view sometimes refer to it as **fulfilment theology**, while its detractors tend to call it **replacement theology**. Those who believe that there are prophecies about Israel remaining to be fulfilled despite Christ's incarnation, believe that there will yet be a central part for Israel as a people and as a nation including a restored land, city and temple. For these Christians the return of Jews to Palestine in 1948 was seen as more than positive justice for a stateless nation: it was the fulfilment of biblical prophecy. Some of those who hold on to a post-Christian Jewish fulfilment of prophecy like this are accused of being the perpetrators of a contemporary form of Judaizing. To them, those who disagree are guilty of a kind of anti-Semitic theology.

What all of us must be agreed about is our gratitude to Israel as a nation and our commitment to being ambassadors of reconciliation to them. They have given us the Old Testament Scriptures and above all they have given us Jesus. Our purpose in this chapter is to recognise the fact that Britain has been deeply anti-Semitic at many times during our history, to uncover the key periods and events, and repent wholeheartedly of it.

From the time of the famine in Egypt, when the Israelites became slaves of Pharaoh, through to the present day, Jews have been hated, feared, discriminated against, enslaved, imprisoned, and murdered. Yet, despite successive attempts to wipe them out in mass genocide or infanticide, the Jewish people have survived as a distinct race. Other civilisations and races under threat have been eliminated, still others have been forced to assimilate. The Jews have retained their identity no matter where they have been scattered throughout the world, and no matter where they have gone they have been able to retain their distinctive worship of God.

The Jewish people still mourn the six million Jews who were killed in the Holocaust during the Second World War, having been taken from nation after nation in Nazi-occupied Europe. Most of us, too, have been overcome with feelings of revulsion as we have witnessed on our TV screens the appalling sight of masses of gaunt bodies, the victims of the gas chambers cast into open graves, or of piles of charred bones, the gruesome remains of the death ovens.

Yet despite this catastrophic persecution, the Jewish people have survived. According to *Operation World*[1] 4.5 million Jews live in the State of Israel – and the numbers are increasing every year through immigration.

Europe has been described as the world's largest Jewish graveyard. For it is not just in this century that anti-Semitism has emerged as such a gross horror, but as we have already seen it was rife at the end of the eleventh century when Crusaders set out to liberate the Holy Land from Jew and Muslim alike (see chapter 4). But anti-Semitism had taken root long before that. Right back in the fourth and fifth centuries Jews were prohibited from proselytising or marrying Christians, constructing new synagogues or receiving compensation if existing ones were burnt down.

Anti-Semitism took root particularly in France during the reign of Charlemagne. Motivated by the desire to avenge the death of a friend, Charlemagne ordered the destruction of the synagogues of Saragossa (along with the mosques) and forced the conversion of worshippers. Throughout the eleventh century church-inspired attacks on Jewish settlements occurred, culminating in a massacre at Rouen. The Crusaders 'herded the Jews into a certain place of worship, rounding them up by force or guile, and without distinction of age or sex put them to the sword. Those who accepted Christianity escaped the sword.'[2]

Britain's anti-Semitism fed off the Crusades. Richard I (the Lion-Heart), who was prominent in the organisation of the third Crusade, helped spread the fever to Britain.

'His coronation in 1189 was attended by the burning of the London Jewry, with the loss of 30 lives. In the months following there were attacks on the Jewish community in several places, particularly in East Anglia, when Kings Lynn, Norwich, Stamford, Bury St Edmunds and Lincoln prepared the way for the death by fire and mass suicide of the Jewish community in York in March 1190.'[3]

That York massacre in 1190 (or mass suicide as it was reported) occurred after Jews were besieged by a fanatical Christian mob.

In 1220 the Jew badge (intended as a badge of shame), so grossly copied by Hitler in the Second World War, was introduced in Britain. The notion of the blood-libel – the idea that Jews killed Jesus, therefore all Jews were the enemies of Christians – became popular and Britain was the first country to carry out 'the final solution', namely the mass expulsion of Jews. For four hundred years, until the time and influence of Cromwell, Jews virtually vanished from British shores. Ethnic cleansing is not a new evil!

During those four hundred years anti-Jewish stereotypes became ingrained in English life through sermons, plays and religious literature. Catholics, Anglicans and even Puritans adopted the demonic medieval image of the Jews as a rejected and despised group.

The word 'Jew' still carries an undertone of scorn and contempt. The stereotypical image of betrayal and conniving commercial ways associated with Jewish people was epitomised, for example, by Shakespeare's Shylock in *The Merchant of Venice*, Marlowe's *The Jew of Malta*, and more recently in some of T.S. Eliot's poetry.

In the twentieth century Jews have been denounced for their 'corrupting' role in public life. They were largely blamed for the Boer War by radicals, who referred to the rich gold merchants of South Africa as the 'Jew-jingo gang' and also accused the 'Jew press' of hoodwinking the British public into supporting the war in the Transvaal.

Between 1918 and 1922 a right-wing anti-Jewish and anti-Zionist campaign of unusual intensity was provoked as a response to the Balfour Declaration of 1917, when Britain committed itself to sponsor a Jewish national home in Palestine. In 1929 Arnold Leese founded the Imperial Fascist League, openly calling for the total expulsion of all Jews from Britain. He went public in saying that he would have preferred 'to exterminate them by some humane method such as the lethal chamber'. Did Hitler first get the idea for his gruesome tortures from Leese?

Most of us would not in any way support or countenance the activities of the National Front, the Imperial Fascist League or the British Union of Fascists. We deplore the racist anti-Jewish slogans heard at football matches, the desecrations of graves in Jewish cemeteries, and the assaults on orthodox Jews.

However, the existence of these minority interest groups surely reflects the tip of an uncomfortable iceberg and the extreme of a general tendency. There are no rational grounds for this prejudice. Underneath it all lies what we term 'a passive anti-Semitism', a kind of social dislike rather than an organised form – a reserve and an unwillingness to be pro-Jewish. Jews themselves recognise that anti-Semitism has been a 'remarkably persistent undercurrent in British society and culture'.[4] Despite the huge contribution Jews have made to international culture and advances in modern thought and science, and despite some prominent Jews who have held recent political office (for example, Sir Leon Brittan, Sir Keith Joseph, Nigel Lawson), 'racism, intolerance and anti-Jewish prejudice continue to exist within a mainstream liberal framework.'[5]

During the Second World War anti-Semitic demands for the internment of refugee Jews fleeing from Nazi persecution were acceded to. Virtually nothing was done to rescue European Jews from the Holocaust. Even after the war only a trickle of Jewish refugees was allowed to enter the country, reflecting 'a lamentable example of British officialdom's callous insensitivity to the Jewish plight.'[6] Adding insult to injury we banished Holocaust survivors to Palestine, and there were even anti-Jewish riots in several British cities. At a time when the concentration camps in Germany were emptying and the Jews were desperately needing their own homeland, the British Navy took active steps to prevent refugees from German camps reaching Israel, even firing on boats carrying refugees and sinking them.

We dragged our heels over the plans and discussions for a Jewish homeland in the years from the end of the Second World War to the foundation of modern Israel in 1948. Had we been less ambivalent we might have contributed more rapidly and positively to a settlement of greater justice for Jews and Palestinians alike. And British Christians are still ambivalent. Our theological differences influence our attitudes towards the Jews. Some are enthusiastically for Jews and Zionism, others are positive towards Jewish evangelism, whereas those who are uncommitted theologically tend to back off from anything that is pro-Jew, so displaying an unspoken anti-Semitism.

We dislike foreigners. We have had our anti-black riots; we have discriminated against immigrants from the West Indies; we still regard non-white ethnic minorities as inferior simply because they are minorities and we still reject them as equals. Even though Jews have lived among us for centuries, we still give them the cold shoulder (and they, for their part, are often quite separatist, like any minority group).

I was attending a barbecue in Reading for newly arrived overseas students. It is something Christians in Reading have been taking the lead in for a while. Every summer there is a new intake of international students which number about 20 per cent of the total student body at Reading University, one of the highest in the country.

I sat chatting to two students, one a Jew from Israel, the other a Muslim from Africa. When they found out I was a committed Christian their attitude changed to suspicion and uncertainty about how to handle me. The Jewish student said, 'You Christians hate us Jews, don't you?' 'Not at all,' I answered. I then went on to tell him that because he was a Jew I felt an unusual respect and love for him, because Jesus Christ was a Jew too. 'He was one of you, born among you and that to me makes you special.' The student's mouth dropped open. I had blown away a misconception he had been brought up on.

How many more Jews carry around this same misconception? Doesn't our past record justify their apprehension? They have sure grounds to fear that we continue to hate them. They hear that because Jesus was a Jew and was put to death by Jews, Jews are hated by all Christians – a throwback to the Crusades and to repeated statements by Church leaders over many generations.

Is it not possible for us to love Jewish people, to pray for them to discover Jesus as their Messiah? Even if we disagree with the more extreme aspects of their political action – and it is usually the extremes we witness on our television screens – we, as God's chosen people too, should be loving them, reaching out to them, befriending them and discussing with

them something we have so much in common with them –
the Old Testament Scriptures.

Luke 13:34 describes Jesus' heart for the city of Jerusalem:

> *'O Jerusalem, Jerusalem ... How often I wanted to gather your*
> *children together, just as a hen gathers her brood under her*
> *wings...'*

Jesus wept over Jerusalem and longed that the city and its
people would be gathered to Him. This is still His desire and
must be ours too.

In a *Daily Telegraph* editorial on 3 January 1994 William
Rees-Mogg wrote:

> 'The Christian churches ought to make some formal act
> of contrition for what has happened over these 2,000
> years; we need not take responsibility for Titus or
> perhaps for the Cossacks, but we do need to apologise
> for the massacres, for the Inquisition, for the ghettoes,
> for the badges, for the expulsions; for the accusations of
> blood guilt, and above all for the Christian failure to
> perceive in time, the full evil of the Holocaust. We do
> not need to sentimentalise the Jews – not all Jews are
> saints, Israel is a self-interested state as others are – but
> we need to accept our responsibility for a history which
> is the exact opposite of the Christian ethic...
>
> Christians must be prepared to recognise what has
> been done to the Jews in the name of their religion.
> Protestants need to reflect on the ultimate implications
> of the German anti-Semitism of Luther; Catholics need
> to reflect on their share in the persecution. Of course,
> there is the other side; there is the splendid statement of
> a 15th-century pope which starts with the words:
> "Whereas the Jews are made to the image of God"; but
> as Christians, who worship a saviour who was a circum-
> cised Jew, we have shared in a history of recurrent
> destruction of the Jewish people.'

So we need to apologise – again and again – for our anti-
Semitism, and for our part in the world's sins against the
Jews. We need to apologise as Christians, and as British

people. When we do so, we will cross the barriers of hate and fear which still divide us.

We need, too, to recognise demonic intent in keeping the Jews a marginalised and hated race. The infanticide at the time of Moses, and by Herod after Jesus was born, the massacres of the Crusades and the Holocaust by Hitler are only public expressions of a continued world-wide, sinister hatred and antagonism that is particularly stirred up by people who are no friends of the Lord, but of Satan himself. We need to oppose Satan's purposes towards the Jew and champion God's.

Notes

1. Patrick Johnstone, *Operation World* (OM Publishing, 1993 edn).
2. J.F. Benton (ed.), *Self and Society in Twelfth-century France: the Memoirs of Abbot Guibert of Nogent* (New York, 1970).
3. R.B. Dobson, *The Jews of Medieval York and the Massacre of March 1190*, Borthwick Papers No. 45 (York, 1974).
4. Robert S. Wistrich, *Anti-Semitism – the Longest Hatred* (Thames/Mandarin, 1992).
5. Ibid., p. 111.
6. Ibid., p. 109.

Chapter 12

The Opium Trade

Few people are aware of quite how badly China has been treated by European nations throughout the last four hundred years. In *The Observer* newspaper of 30 June 1996 Andrew Higgins outlined 'Four hundred years of shame: the long march of Chinese humiliation'. In this article he detailed thirteen significant episodes including:

- *1513* The first Europeans, Portuguese, set foot on Chinese soil.

- *1556–7* The Chinese agreed to rent Portuguese merchants the peninsula now called Macao and never formally ceded to Portugal.

- *1620s* Portuguese landed on Taiwan renaming it Formosa; later they made way for the Spanish and Dutch to move in.

- *1839–42* First Opium War between Britain and China which Britain won and which led to the Treaty of Nanking, opening up five cities to foreign trade: Canton, Frizhon, Amoy, Ningpo and Shanghai and ceding Hong Kong to Britain.

- *1858* The second Opium War also won by Britain which led to the Treaty of Tientsin in which the Chinese agreed to stop calling the British *cyi* (barbarians) and allowed them a permanent ambassador in Beijing. The Beijing Convention then ceded the Kowloon peninsular opposite Hong Kong island to Britain.

- *1884* The French fleet sank China's southern fleet in less than an hour. China then assented to French claims in Indo-China. Subsequently, Japan wiped out the Chinese northern fleet at Weihaiwei. Two Chinese admirals and one Qing official committed suicide.

- *1898–9* The Germans used an attack on missionaries to seize Qingdao and claim mining and railway rights. The British seized Weihaiwei and were granted a ninety-nine year lease on the New Territories. The Russians occupied a Manchman port.

- *1900* A twenty-thousand-strong force from Japan, Russia, Britain and the USA was sent to quell the Chinese anti-foreign rebellion. China agreed to allow permanent foreign guards to protect the foreign quarter in perpetuity and to pay an indemnity of £67 million which was twice the entire imperial revenue.

In the face of this catalogue of injustices it is hardly surprising that China is today one of the most fiercely anti-Western nations. The fact that it has one of the fastest-growing Churches on earth is among the best evidence of the supernatural grace of God. The fact that among the worst offenders against China were the British underscores once again the vulnerability of Britain to the judgement of God.

There is no way that our dealings with China can be explained apart from the primacy of greed in our colonial enterprise. This was precisely the motivation of the two Opium Wars. They were waged by Britain against China to enforce the opening of Chinese ports to trade in opium. Opium from British India paid for Britain's imports from China, such as porcelain, silk, and above all, tea. This trade was promoted by the British East India Company. Indeed the colonial history of China and India is deeply interrelated because of the role of the East India Company in forming that history.

The East India Company began its life as a private merchant trading company in 1600 but in 1834, when its charter ran out, its activities were continued by the British Government in tandem with the private merchants of the day and it became the arm of imperial power. However, its intimate relationship with the British Government had its seeds right back in its early days when, on Charles II's wedding to the Portuguese Catharine of Braganza, Bombay was 'acquired' as a marriage settlement. Charles gave Bombay to the East India Company and it became a base for trade with China. In 1711, England acquired a trading post in Canton when the emperor relaxed the trading rules. The East India Company by this time had leased Madras and Calcutta from Indian princes and also gained control of Bengal. We have already dealt with some of these issues in more detail as they affected India (see chapter 6). Suffice it to say that Noam Chomsky in *Year 501* cites Clive as describing the Bengal area in the mid-eighteenth century as 'extensive, populous and rich as the city of London'.[1] He goes on to quote Adam Smith who was writing in the latter part of the same century, only twenty years later, 'three or four hundred thousand people die of hunger in one year'. These are the consequences of the 'improper regulations' and 'injudicious restraints' imposed by the ruling Company upon the rice trade, which turned 'dearth into a famine'. The text continues:

> 'It has not been uncommon [for Company officials] when the chief foresaw that extraordinary profit was likely to be made by opium [to plough up] a rich field of rice or other grain ... in order to make room for a plantation of poppies.'[2]

However, at the same time as Adam Smith was writing these words in the 1770s, the East India Company was in financial difficulties because it was unable to obtain enough silver to cover its trade deficit. Export of tea and silk from China was expanding but import of British goods was remaining constant. As a result the Company was over-stretched and outstripped its banking facilities. It was unable to pay its debts to the Bank of England or Customs and Excise. The British Government had to bail the company out to the tune of £1.4 million. This gives a clue as to how lucrative the tea trade was to the British Government in duty and how important it was for them that the trade should continue. In order to meet the trade deficit and secure future profits the East India Company deliberately stimulated the production of opium. By 1781 they had actually assumed the responsibility for its production in India. They tended to avoid actually shipping into China themselves but instead sold it on the Calcutta market to Indian traders who smuggled it to China for disposal. In other words it was a back-door trade. These traders were non-British as the East India Company had the monopoly of British trade between India and China. After 1793 this monopoly was lifted and other British merchants carried on the trade.

The impact of the opium on China was dreadful. By the early 1800s the drug had penetrated deep into the Chinese interior. It reached Beijing and into the palace of the emperor himself, enslaving members of his bodyguard and his court eunuchs. As the century went on the opium habit bit sharply into the army and into the children of the wealthy and powerful. The Chinese Emperor Tao-Kuang is said to have lost his three eldest sons from opium addiction.

The trade was not without its serious opponents at home, as was to be expected during a period of so much revival, social reform and missionary endeavour. In 1830 a House of Commons' Committee of Enquiry was set up to scrutinise the affairs of the Company, but this was easily disarmed by a mixture of lies and bogus argument. The Company line was that it had to retain its monopoly of the opium trade in order to keep prices high enough to restrict the 'non-medical' demand. But the real issue was economics. The opium trade with China was worth over two million pounds annually which in those days was almost half the amount it cost to service the Crown and the Civil Service. The Government's way out was to curtail the activities of the Company and take on direct responsibility for the future opium trade between India and China. Throughout the ensuing century the trade went from strength to strength. By 1859 it was 60,000 chests a year and by 1880 it was 105,000, the majority coming from British India. The Chinese addict population is said to have been in excess of fifteen million by this time.

This is not to say that senior British Government leaders did not speak out against it. In the 1840s, after the first Opium War, Gladstone strongly condemned the drug trade in the House of Commons and called for a prohibition of the cultivation of the poppy in India. He said of the first Opium War, 'a war more unjust in its origins, a war more calculated in its progress to lower this country with permanent disgrace, I do not know and have not read of.' Yet, a few years later he accepted the imposition of an import duty on opium – tantamount to acknowledging it as an acceptable commodity. The economic power of the trade proved irresistible to the British Government throughout the century, as indeed it also did to the Chinese Government but in a quite reverse manner.

The Chinese Government, the Qing dynasty, opposed the trade from the start. As far back as 1729 when the Portuguese were importing the opium, the emperor had ordered all imports to be stopped. But the decree had little impact. At first the British had a licence from the Chinese to import, but it was too narrow for her agents the East India Company, as we have seen, and so the Company arranged for it to be smuggled in. The Chinese Government tried everything to eradicate the trade. They tried flogging and publicly shaming addicts; they tried exiling and executing them. In the 1830s they considered legalising the drug so as to do away with any need for a black market and smuggling. But instead they decided in 1839 to go to the root of the problem. Most trafficking took place via Canton. A provincial viceroy by the name of Lin Tse Hsu was appointed to arrest the smugglers, send all their ships home, and forbid and prevent any further imports. British merchants were ordered to surrender 20,000 chests containing approximately 140 lbs of opium each. These chests were polluted with salt and lime, and flushed into the sea. The idea was to clean up the customs service, but the enormously high profitability of the trade meant that high levels of bribes were offered by the smugglers which continued to corrupt the customs service. In any case the British Government took great exception to 'the most shameful violence' done to the trade and traders. In June 1840 an expeditionary force conducted the first Opium War which simply served to open up more cities to the trade. In the following decade the trade doubled. The next emperor took even stronger measures against the trade including beheading or enslaving persistent users. Finally another official was appointed, Yeh Ming-Chen. But by now the British could see the advantages to be had in opening up even more ports to trade in general, and was looking for a reason to demonstrate a show of military power and force another treaty. In 1856 a smuggling ship carrying a British flag was apprehended off Canton. Yeh Ming-Chen refused to back down or apologise so the navy shelled his official residence. Palmerston called an election on the issue which he won with a patriotic mandate for a second Opium War. This ended in eleven more ports being opened to Western trade. Once again the trade in opium almost doubled.

By this time the Chinese gave in to the trade with the conclusion that the only way to overcome the external dependence was to grow it themselves (which they had hardly if ever done, apart from for medicinal purposes, so great was their opposition to the drug). The wheel began to turn full circle and by the beginning of the twentieth century the drug which had been pushed onto China by the Western Europeans and particularly the British began to find its way back to Britain where up until now it had been restricted to medical and therapeutic use. Now there was public outcry that such a drug should threaten the youthful social élite and the British working man. Here lie the roots of contemporary heroin addiction in the United Kingdom.

It is our conviction that the demonic strongholds that were built between Britain and China and between Britain and India by this evil trade can be exposed and dealt with by the blood of the cross of Christ and some of the bondage of drug addiction in these countries be broken. This is not to claim easy victories but to recognise that demonic powers infest both drug trade and addiction, having gained access through past injustice and malpractice. These are what gave it its special hold then and give it its special hold even now. While identificational repentance today may not affect the current traffickers directly, it will, we believe, displace enough of the powers rooted in our colonial past to give greater advantage to those seeking freedom from addiction and gain advantage over the perpetrators of the trade today. We really have no right to speak out against drug trafficking from North Africa, South America and Asia today, if we are not prepared as a nation to take the blame for the way in which we initially created the demand.

Fortunately we have the prayers, sacrificial work and anointings of past men and women who opposed the trade throughout colonial times as a foundation to build on. The Society for the Suppression of the Opium Trade, for example, functioned throughout the last twenty years or so of the nineteenth century and published a monthly magazine *The Friend of China*. They conducted meetings throughout the country and particularly exposed and opposed the spurious findings of the Royal Commission on the Opium Trade in 1895. Our friend, Kate Young, had a great-grandfather who was a medical missionary in Bengal throughout the last two decades of the nineteenth century. She has in her possession some revealing correspondence between her relative, Dr Donald Morison, and a Mr Matheson of *The Friend of China* dated 2 May 1895:

'My dear Dr Morison,

The Royal Commission on opium is acting in a very tricky way and the Indian Govt. are doing all they can to get the British public to accept their conclusions. We are going to do all we can and with prayer to God to counteract their attempt to hoodwink the Public.

Sir Joseph Pease ballotted with the hope of getting a day to discuss the subject and providentially has secured a day 24th May for the debate. On the 22nd we are to have a great Anti-opium meeting.

You may be interested in seeing a copy of Mr Rowntrees' pamphlet on "The opium habit in the East". I send it but the main defect of the Commission's report is their careful omission of any reference to China.'

Another friend was involved in the publication of a book about two amazing world-travelling missionary women of the same period: Katherine Bushnell and Elizabeth Andrew who worked with the Women's Christian Temperance Union. In its day this was a powerful organisation working on a range of social issues. They had direct access to Government. Behind their activities as reformers was a life of prayer. A quotation from this book states:

' ... the fact that children as young as seven were kept in training in opium dens and houses of prostitution, and the "Christian" officers of the Protectorate would do nothing to secure the children's release, was an utter condemnation of Christianity as far as the Chinese were concerned.' [3]

Missionaries from the China Inland Mission were at the forefront of opposition to the trade. Writing in *The Friend of China* Leonard Star writes:

' ... we are told that it is now too late – that whatever there has been of error or of sin in the past is beyond recall, and that even if we did force opium into China at the cannon's mouth in bygone days, we can never hope to successfully suppress it now that the Chinese grow it for themselves. But surely our duty – that thing so sacred, or supposed to be in every Englishman's eyes – is plain. "It is never too late to mend", and we can stop our part in the infamous traffic of – is it too strong an expression for the case? – "the souls of men" and cease the growth and sale of opium in India, whence it is weekly taken in enormous quantities to China, having been prepared in a special way to suit the Chinese market. I know from experience that the nauseous smell of the prepared drug comes up from the holds of vessels under the British flag plying between the East and the Far East.'

We need to play our part in bringing to its culmination the hard work of past prophets and intercessors and deal with the spiritual backlog left by these sins of the nations.

Notes

1. South End Press, 1995.
2. Ibid., p. 12.
3. Dene Hardwick, *Oh Thou Woman That Bringest Good Tidings* (Christians for Biblical Equality).

Chapter 13

North American Settlements

On too many occasions have we been in conversation or in meetings where Americans have been the butt of criticism. They are usually criticised for being pushy, arrogant, insensitive – and more talented than the British! Even well-known Christian leaders like Billy Graham and John Wimber have been on the receiving end of criticism about their American methods. Often Christian leaders from across the Atlantic have felt this antagonism deeply, and have not understood why it is there. We are quick to criticise American predominance at conferences, in ideas, personnel and cultural superiority. We comment disparagingly about 'tele-evangelists', American-style cults, corruption in politics, race relations, the prevalence of violence and a host of other things we profess to dislike about the American way of life. We even joke about their tendency to systematise new understanding and initiatives into manuals, whilst we form committees!

We rarely see the positive. The fact that of all the Western nations they have poured far more resources and personnel into missions, that they have been the first into new fields of opportunity, the first to bale out struggling nations, the first to help Europe out after the Second World War, the first to initiate global conferences and partnerships, seems to pass us by unnoticed. Why is it that we are so grudging as Christians towards them? Why are we so slow to affirm them for their generous spirit? Why are we so quick to criticise and condemn, yet so slow to welcome and encourage them? Can it be that we see too much of what we dislike about ourselves mirrored in them? Are we rather like the parents of a child who, after leaving home to make her way in a far country, returns home to declare with pride all that she has accomplished – without reference to and without the help of her parents? We ought to thank God that Americans, so many of whom **are** our offspring, have succeeded where we haven't, have done so well on the world stage, and have contributed so much by way of new initiatives and understanding.

America is not an easy nation for outsiders to fathom. More than any other nation in the world, it is a nation of immigrants. Large numbers of different ethnic groups have made their home there. In Miami Spanish is the *lingua franca*, yet in the far north-east, English is spoken with an English accent! There are large concentrations of Latins from many nations. It is home to West Indians, Filipinos and Chinese. Nine point four per cent of the population are Hispanics, 3 per cent Asian Pacifics, 4.2 per cent Jews, Arabs, Armenians and Iranians, 12.1 per cent Afro-Americans, and 0.8 per cent native Americans (Indians) in over 250 ethnic groups, and 70 per cent Euro-Americans. It receives 670,000 legal immigrants annually and 700,000 illegal ones![1] It is a microcosm of the whole world. So when we criticise, we are in danger of criticising ourselves and our offspring.

It is also essentially a Christian nation, with 86.5 per cent of the population professing faith! Evangelicals comprise 30 per cent of the faith community, and Pentecostals and Charismatics 13.4 per cent. Twenty-three per cent of the Protestant congregations of the world are located in the USA (1993 figures) and 52 per cent of the world's Protestant missionary force are American – a figure which of course is rapidly changing, as God works so powerfully in what were the traditional 'fields' for American missionaries – Korea, Philippines, and Latin America.

In chapter 1, we told the story of the Gideon's Army prayer conference in Korea in 1993 and recalled the impact on us of the Americans' repentance of the sins of their forefathers as white immigrants against the native American Indians during the settlement period of American history. Over the past few years there have been many moving, powerful and very relevant acts of repentance by Americans towards the different people groups within their nation. John Dawson's book *Healing America's Wounds*[2] gives many examples. We ourselves have participated in such acts of reconciliation in America, and praise God for the many repercussions these have had in continued healing of relationships between estranged groups, denominations, races and tribes. We have rejoiced too at the way that political statements and action have sometimes followed closely on the heels of these acts of confession and reconciliation, and at the many break-throughs of blessing the nation has experienced.

The USA is still rejoicing over recent and current revivals, like the College revivals, the movement of God at Pensacola and Baltimore, the masses of men congregating in the 'Promise-keepers' movement, and the turning to God in many Indian tribal reservations. Christians have been at the forefront of dealing with explosions of racial and ethnic violence in places like Los Angeles and Boston and reacting to the emergence of private militias. America has led the way in encouraging a global movement of prayer of outstanding and possibly unprecedented proportions. Within the United States millions are committing themselves to city-wide prayer concerts, to early-morning prayer, to Marches for Jesus and to a whole host of new prayer initiatives.

America is certainly an interesting place to be. As else-where in the world it is sometimes a volatile place to be. But what has made it so particularly volatile – apart from the obvious fact that so many people groups living side by side is always a recipe for ethnic eruption? We believe that part of the answer lies in European involvement, and more specific-ally English involvement, in American history – particularly during the settlement period in the seventeenth century, when America was founded and settled by a miscellany of groups and interests. Soldiers, traders, and separatist Chris-tians (the Pilgrim Fathers) fleeing from 'the King's Church', arrived on the *Mayflower* and the other ships that followed. Later came convicts banished from England and slaves brought from Africa. Colonists from Holland, France, Spain, Germany and Scandinavia also contributed towards what has been termed 'the invasion of America', as did Christian groups, fleeing persecution in Europe, who came to establish their Utopia in the New World – among them the Amish, the Mennonites, and the Huguenots. Each group, from whatever country they came, brought with them their own culture, their own nationality, their own language – a parochialism of their very own. Those who came from Britain even brought the distinct characteristics of their own particular district. From wherever each group of settlers came they carried with them their own nation's prevailing morals and value systems.

A plethora of Christian denominations was established – all the Protestant ones existing at that time in Western Europe, and many more were created as the separatist spirit continued to thrive and splinter into myriads of tiny denominations. The seeds of division don't disappear when we separate from a church – they are carried with us and they reproduce themselves. That is why reconciliation is so powerful, in that it begins to counteract these divisions and create a climate for co-operation. There was both the good – the search for truth and godliness, and missionary zeal – and the bad. The breaking from Rome's hierarchical monopoly may have released forces that we still don't understand.

It was a violent era and an adventurous one. To set sail to discover new lands and a new way of life required a courageous pioneer spirit and a tenacious instinct for survival. All of this and more has contributed to make what America is today. Much of what emerged has been good – but not all.

When these settlers arrived many of them established their own separatist colonies on confined stockades and sought to become self-sufficient, self-reliant and self-defensive. They formed their own militias – they had to in order to survive. Many of the idealists arrived with strong Christian principles, but were forced to adjust their values in order to accommodate their new way of life. Unfortunately, within a generation or two we find Christian groups becoming involved in bloodshed. The Puritans engaged in the conquest of Indian tribes. Treaties were made and broken. Trading agreements were coercive and exploitive. The native Indians were treated as inferior pagans. Land was taken, some of it forcibly. Disagreements, disputes and differing approaches became commonplace. The battle lines were drawn.

Some understood that battle to be between civilisation and savagery; others between the Old Testament Protestant model of Christianity and heathenism; others considered it to be about true racism, between white and red, and later between white and black, lords and slaves – the feudal model from the Normans. Some viewed their coming to New England as another Crusade (the Roman Catholic model), and felt sanctified as the early Crusaders had done in their desire to liberate the Promised Land. 'Civilisation was the property of the divinely-chosen people of New England' (William Hubbard). Values were often shaped by inadequate doctrine, and doctrine, as always, was coloured by prevailing thinking and practice.

Francis Jennings, in *The Invasion of America*, writes:

> 'When Europeans began their astounding voyages to "dazzling new worlds", they could carry only the freight they possessed; the ideas and institutions with which they conquered and colonized were the same they knew at home. Europeans used the technology of superior ships and guns to gain beach-heads, they then imposed on top of indigenous societies the devices best understood by the conquerors.'[3]

The legacy they brought with them was of the destruction of whole communities by peoples marching in arms. In 1578 Queen Elizabeth I authorised Sir Humphrey Gilbert to seize remote heathen and barbarous lands, and spoke at length of imposition of government and the seizure of property. In the Government's mind was the launch of the English Empire. Five years later Gilbert received a charter, which referred to 'the compassion of God for these poor infidels, it seeming probable that God hath reserved these Gentiles to be introduced into Christian civility by the English nation.'[4] Some Protestant Reformers, on the other hand, brought with them a fear and hatred of infidels. The Crusader period had informed them of the need to exterminate or enslave the infidel.

'Some part of the ideas of Elizabethan English colonizers were brought to America from their previous experience in Ireland. These adventurers had gone to Ireland with a preconceived idea of a barbaric society and they merely tailored the Irishman to fit this ideological strait-jacket. They then used the same pretexts for the extermination of the Indians as their counterparts had used in the 1560s and 1570s for the slaughter of numbers of the Irish.'[5]

Intriguingly, Sir Thomas Smythe who was treasurer of the Virginia Company from 1609 to 1620, held that post simultaneously with the post of governor of the East India Company. The Virginia Company was eventually disbanded by the Government because funds collected in England for the establishment of a college to train Indians in Christianity had been misused by the Company and its employees 'for other purposes'.

In the southern state of Virginia early settlers founded Jamestown, although at the end of the first year only thirty-eight of the original one hundred and four survived. This settlement was founded on an entirely different set of values to the pilgrim fathers – primarily a desire for wealth and empowerment.

'The Virginia Company was comprised of London entre-preneurs who formed a joint stock company, a venture in which investors pooled their capital and shared the risks of business. From the beginning there were bitter battles and struggles for company control in London, bitter disputes among the colonists and conflict with the Indians. Immigrants eventually began to pour in, drawn by cheap or free land and the profits that could be gained from an addictive weed named tobacco.'[6]

The first black slaves arrived in Virginia as early as 1619. Religion was paid lip service initially – it wasn't until Wesley's era that Methodism began to pervade society.

In the northern states of New England, however, it was principally the Christian separatists from Europe who settled the region. 'The people of the north sought freedom to worship as they pleased. They clustered in small farming communities centred on the church, where they sought to win a living from the soil. They wanted a thrifty, independ-ent, "godly" life.'[7]

The difference between the North and the South couldn't have been more marked. This divide was principally between the 'Anglos' – the Christian North and the non-Christian South – and these eventually became the divisions that gave rise to the American Civil War. However, the blame for all the worst aspects of the white man's activity was laid at the door of the Church since it was Christian people who had colonised the area, but who, within a generation, had shown the same sinful qualities as their English forebears.

The need for funds and worthwhile trade also affected the Christians. The Saints of Plymouth, Massachusetts, showed how to wipe out a competitor forcefully without exposing themselves to the crown's justice. The trick was to manipulate the Indians so as to achieve their aims, while diverting blame to the savages. On one occasion, discovering an Indian 'conspiracy', a contingent of soldiers from the Plymouth plantation marched to save some fellow colonists, who weren't in danger. They then enticed some Indians into their hands and slaughtered them. The Plymouth Saints were not quite Puritans, but to Indian eyes they seemed to be in agreement with the other settlers on all things and so they were branded the same. The root of the problem lies in the fact that, wherever the gospel has gone, even those who have been pure in doctrine and motivation, have been equated with the less scrupulous, those who profess to come as Christians with a Christian message, but adopt a suspect methodology.

On many occasions the trading needs in both North and South led to deceitful practice, the breaking of agreements with fellow colonists, and the playing off of Indians against them, leading to open conflicts and bloodshed. Again and again greed and unrighteous trade led to war and further division. The Indians became scapegoats for every kind of supposed evil. They were discriminated against, plundered, their villages set alight, and their women and children put to death.

The imposition of slavery on the plantations created new injustices. Treated as inferior pagans, many slaves suffered cruelly at the hands of their masters.

'The thirty million Afro-American community is a victim of its origins in slavery and discrimination. The civil rights movement achieved much in changing structures and attitudes, but the cycle of unemployment, poverty, family instability and crime is unbroken for many.

Native Americans have suffered intensely in their encounter with centuries of European immigrants. They have lost almost all their lands, their self-respect and much of their culture, and they still face prejudice and insensitivity to their plight.'[8]

They too have suffered in exactly the same way as the natives of all too many lands we English have colonised.

In a thesis 'The Principality over the Massachusetts Bay', Michael Courtney traces the development of the settlements. The Pilgrims arrived at Plymouth in 1620, followed by the Puritans at Salem in 1629. Both groups were fleeing persecution from the Church of England in the immediate post-Reformation period. The Pilgrims were separatists and disapproved of the monarch taking the title of 'Head of the Church'. The Puritans were hoping to purify the Church of England from within, but the leaders of that Church, not recognising the need for purification, oppressed those who were sympathetic to the Puritan cause. Both Pilgrims and Puritans ended up being persecuted, but both had positive ideals – the hope of bringing Christ's light to the pagans in the New World.

The Puritans were Calvinists, deeply concerned for holiness and discipline, and hungering and thirsting after righteousness. 'Given the noble beginnings of the early settlements, one is left wondering what happened. How did Massachusetts become the den of wickedness that it is today? The seeds of failure were sown within the first two generations of settlers.'[9] The weakness in their Calvinism – and their human frailty – were found out. Initially, when drought, disease or disasters affected them, they would cry out to God and engage in repentance. But 'they became superficial and perfunctory in their repentance and would turn away from God a little sooner each time' – like the children of Israel (and many modern Christians!).

Two things compromised their faith in the eyes of others: the shedding of the blood of Indians in armed confrontation, and their desire for economic prosperity.

They gained prosperity primarily through trade and shipping, so that making money rather than meeting needs became the chief purpose of their merchant-centred economy.

'The danger that the commercial spirit would defeat the intentions of the founders was early foreseen. Long before the end of the seventeenth century the commercial spirit began to triumph, subtly moderating and modifying the attitude of the colony towards its neighbours. By the time the first generation had passed away the theocracy had given way to a plutocracy, and the economic interests of the colony were fast obscuring the ideals of the founders.' [10]

Scripture tells us that *'the love of money is a root of all sorts of evil'* (1 Timothy 6:10). Over and over again this is seen as the root English sin against the nations, and the reason for every other subterfuge, atrocity, betrayal, intimidation, injustice and crime.

It can be argued that surely the early settlers are responsible for their own sin. Each of us can be led astray by the enemy of our souls. We can be compromised by the prevailing spirit of the age. We are each responsible for the actions we take in a sinful way, and the attitudes we display. Yes, that is surely right. But that is not the whole truth. There is another element in the need for reconciliation between the English (or British) and Americans. Euro-Americans have been at the fore in confessing the sins of their forefathers towards the Indians. They are diligently seeking to face up to their own internal guilt. But has our own responsibility for being involved in that process, for being the cause of so much division in society, and for the continuing bad Anglo-American attitudes, been taken away because those settlers crossed the Atlantic? How affected were they by the prevailing spirit in this country? A sense of rejection by fellow-Christians prompted their bold decision to move to a New World. The spirit of empire and trade influenced their attitudes. How much of all that was because they were English, affected by their upbringing and environment, and how much merely because of the temptations and trials they faced along the way? The writings of James seem to be really appropriate in this consideration.

> *'Listen, my beloved brethren: did not God choose the poor of this world to be rich in faith and heirs of the kingdom which He promised to those who love Him? But you have dishonoured the poor man. Is it not the rich who oppress you and personally drag you into court? Do they not blaspheme the fair name by which you have been called? If, however, you are fulfilling the royal law, according to the Scripture, "You shall love your neighbour as yourself," you are doing well. But if you show partiality, you are committing sin and are convicted by the law as transgressors. For whoever keeps the whole law and yet stumbles in one point, he has become guilty of all. For He who said, "Do not commit adultery," also said, "Do not commit murder." Now if you do not commit adultery, but do commit murder, you have become a transgressor of the law.'* (James 2:5–11)

Notice how this passage addresses groups of people: brethren, the rich, the poor, transgressors – there is therefore a need to address our sin corporately.

Since it was with this very issue that God first began to impact us about reconciliation we feel there need to be significant acts of repentance and reconciliation between the British and the Americans – that is white, Anglo-Saxon Euro-Americans, as well as the ethnic groups that we treated unjustly. We view what the settlers in America did as a reflection of our own selves, as Englishmen. We see today some of their more extreme failings as a distorted mirror of what we as Britishers are – proud and arrogant.

> *'God is opposed to the proud, but gives grace to the humble.'* (James 4:6, 1 Peter 5:5)

During the Thirteen Colonies Prayer Journey which took place in 1997, I joined the team for the New England section. In many of the situations we visited I 'stood in the gap' as an Englishman for the sins committed by my forefathers when this was an English colony. These sins had left a corporate wound which could still be detected in the attitudes prevailing in North American life. One place we went to was Natick – the site of a 'praying village' and the scene of a great betrayal of Christian Indians by Puritan settlers. A missionary, John

Elliot, had been used by God to convert many native Indians, and to help them in many social ways. At one time there were fourteen of these praying villages of Indians, mostly from one tribe, the Nipmuck. They were loyal to the colonists, who had brought them the gospel, helping them with their trekking and giving them information on the whereabouts of other less friendly tribes. The Nipmuck were traditionally at odds with the Mohawk tribe. When King Philip's War against the New Englanders erupted in 1675, the Mohawks along with other tribes joined forces but the Nipmuck and the praying villages remained loyal to the English Puritans. However, they betrayed that loyalty. The inhabitants of the praying villages – about 1100 in all – were rounded up and despatched by canoe and other craft to Deer Island – a remote and inhospitable piece of land in Massachusetts Bay, the equivalent of a concentration camp. It was winter and the majority of that group died of hunger or cold, since inadequate provision was made for them.

Ever since, hundreds of native Americans from many parts of the United States assemble annually at Natick to take the 'journey of tears' down that river to Deer Island. I knelt, wept and prayed and asked forgiveness of God for the sins of my forefathers – English Christian against Indian Christian. More recently I visited Deer Island with about 100 other Americans, including a descendant of the Nipmuck tribe – herself an intercessor. There we spent some time in 'identificational repentance' and taking communion together. We confessed our forefathers' sins as Christians against these fellow Christians and asked for forgiveness. We bound ourselves to each other with a red cord – a symbol of the blood of Christ (and a reminder of Rahab's salvation from Jericho). The event was described by one prayer leader as the most powerful and important time of prayer he had ever been involved in.

What does all this do? It deals with the ancient hatreds. It removes the guilt and shame of the past, and it clears the blockages so that God can work once again in groups previously at variance with one another.

Today we need a humility of spirit towards our American brothers and sisters, and a willingness to identify with them in the sins they are being convicted of. And we need to acknowledge before God the prevailing sin of our forefathers in the Church who, in rejecting and persecuting them, forced them to go out from these shores with the wrong attitudes that have created so many of the problems that plague American society today. We can't change the past, but we can change the present and therefore the effects of the past. Wouldn't it be wonderful, for example, if Christians in Britain had a refined and purified attitude to the Americans in our midst, many of whom have come here as missionaries, wish to partner with us in reaching the lost of our nation and other nations, but still find themselves being rejected as their forefathers had been? They have so much to offer.

Fifteen years ago a man called David Schroeder lived in my home town of Wokingham. He and his family had come here as missionaries. They were part of the Christian and Missionary Alliance – one of the biggest American missionary agencies, with nearly 2,000 congregations in the United States and a church-planting reputation worldwide of the highest order. But here, in England, his mission is hardly known, has always struggled and has but a few churches. They were quality people. We became very good friends and prayer partners. He was leading a small Alliance church in the area, but I always felt he ought to be in a more challenging situation, he was so gifted. The other church leaders in our town didn't really accept him. One or two openly criticised him. He ended up working with and for me at the Evangelical Alliance for a while, but because he was not English, the role he was given was less than he was capable of. Eventually he and his family went back to the States. There he has had many significant responsibilities, which have included being Principal (they called him President) of two Theological Seminaries (including the prestigious NYACK College of New York), and head of the Bible-use Department for his whole denomination. His wife took another degree course and ended up as the personal assistant of James Dobson of Focus on the Family. I've often wondered how big a contribution they could have made to this nation and its spiritual life, had they been given a suitable opening. But we didn't have a place for them. How many more must feel like they must have felt – rejected, devalued, misunderstood and misplaced, and have therefore, like their forefathers before them, gone to the Americas to make their way in life?

We have given a welcome to and been much blessed by the ministry of Billy Graham and the late John Wimber. Yet there have been many voices raised against them, their methods, their back-up – the same kind of voices that are suspicious of the motives of American evangelists. Often these negative voices have been very wounding. Were these the same kind of attitudes that prevailed against the prophetic-type initiators and entrepreneurs of the past? Attitudes that devalued new initiatives and ideas, persecuted their spokesmen, and eventually caused them to flee? Are we still stifling new life and vision and rejecting our best?

Notes

1. Figures from *Operation World* by Patrick Johnstone (OM Publishing, 1993).
2. Regal Books, 1994.
3. Published by W.W. Norton, 1975.
4. Stephen Neill, *A History of Christian Missions* (Pelican, 1964), p. 225.
5. Nicholas P. Canny, *The Ideology of English Colonization; from Ireland to America*, quoted in Jennings, *The Invasion of America*, p. 46.
6. John Dawson, *Healing America's Wounds*, p. 44.
7. Michael Courtney, 'The Principality over the Massachusetts Bay', unpublished thesis.
8. Patrick Johnstone, *Operation World*, pp. 565, 6.
9. Courtney, 'The Principality over the Massachusetts Bay', p. 15.
10. H.E. Hart, *Commonwealth History of Massachusetts*, Volumes 1 and 2 (1927).

Chapter 14

Back Home on our Doorstep

People from other countries often get confused. They refer to England as Britain or the United Kingdom. Many English people are equally confused. They think of themselves as British. Their 'Englishness' is hardly ever a subject of conversation. The Scots, on the other hand, know differently. They are Scots first and British second. The Welsh too have a very strong national identity.

Of course, cultural and language differences have an important part to play in these contrasting outlooks. The Welsh and Gaelic languages, with their rich heritage and deep national significance, are very much alive in their respective countries. Historical influences too are highly relevant. England is not a country of thoroughbreds. As we have already described in chapter 3, it has been invaded over the centuries again and again. In the last half-century – an era of travel – a new 'invasion' has taken place: ethnic groups from many nations have come here! The idea of finding a pure-bred Englishman or woman is becoming increasingly absurd. Paradoxically, however, one still finds people passionately declaring their loyalty to their region or county rather than their country: 'I'm from Yorkshire,' or '...Lancashire'; 'I'm a Kentish man' or '...an East Anglian'; 'I'm Cornish' or '...Cumbrian'. So the English, as a 'mongrel' people, don't really know who they are. This subconscious confusion makes it difficult for them to respond to Scottish, Welsh and Irish antagonism.

Northern Ireland is not geographically part of Great Britain, yet its people recognise themselves as British – more so, it sometimes seems, than those from Britain itself. However Northern Ireland, unlike the Republic of Ireland, is part of the United Kingdom. Then we have the geographical description 'the British Isles', a comprehensive term without any political significance, embracing each of the countries so far mentioned and also including the Channel Islands and the Isle of Man, with their own governments. The description is disliked by the Irish because they aren't 'British'!

So we are the United Kingdom – but are not really 'united', given the differences in temperament, politics and culture. We are four nations, but one state. And we are Great Britain (unless you are Irish), but yet are not really 'great' any more.

'Nationalism is especially dangerous in the United Kingdom, which unites four nationalities, English, Scottish, Welsh and Irish. It risks splitting the kingdom. Nationalism is not, as those who hold it argue, a matter of protecting British interests; it is a religious belief for which the Union Jack or the Cross of St George becomes the religious emblem.' [1]

Are flags becoming religious emblems? Familiar scenes on the terraces of football or rugby matches bear testimony to these words, as do the more chilling scenes from the politics of Ireland where those who carry the Irish tricolour proclaim they are truly Irish and Catholic while those who own British loyalties carry the Union Jack and are Protestant.

They reflect the tensions simmering below the surface of late twentieth-century life which have emerged in the establishment of a Scottish Parliament and a Welsh National Assembly, and the never-to-be forgotten question over Northern Ireland and the cry for that elusive lasting peace – modern tensions which reflect and expose the real antagonisms of yesterday. Can we ever escape the burdens of our history and the legacy it has left us?

How can we understand ourselves?

Ireland

'The sin of England is Ireland', someone recently said to us. There is a long history of bloodshed, Penal Laws, land robbery, intimidation, coercion, injustice and antagonism.

Modern generations have witnessed thirty years of conflict and terrorism, resulting in the deaths of 3,100, with injuries to 36,000 people, through bombings and bullets, the majority being innocent victims. Violent intimidation has forced 60,000 people to move home. At the time of writing, the 'Peace Process', welcomed in a referendum by the people of Northern Ireland, has still to be implemented. These antagonisms have been there for at least four hundred years, and some would say for much longer. Why has there been such long-term hostility, and can it ever end? Will 'peace' be anything more than another temporary respite in the repetitive cycle of conflict?

Like many other smaller nations, Ireland has been a beleaguered land. But unlike other nations, where the aggressor has changed from century to century, Ireland's aggressor has consistently been England. Crucial too has been the inextricable link of religion to the changing fortunes of Ireland. 'Sectarianism', which typically involves the mingling of religion with other factors, characterises the deep-seated feelings present in both Catholic and Protestant communities in Northern Ireland. 'Over the centuries both bloodshed and imbalance of interest pervaded the text of Irish/English relations, imbalance as a constant theme and bloodshed as an all too frequent punctuation.'[2]

In order to get to grips with the situation it is perhaps helpful to know that there were two early strands of Christianity introduced to these islands. Undoubtedly, with the Roman conquest there came some Christian influence, maybe through converted slaves and soldiers. Both slaves and soldiers were present in the early Middle Eastern Church. The early Roman Church had bishops in England, but their influence failed to spread to the outlying regions of Britain. So Wales, Scotland and Ireland successfully resisted Roman occupation (hence Hadrian's Wall) and Roman church life. Throughout the Roman occupation of the British mainland, which lasted four hundred years, no Roman pattern of organisation, administration or influence was imposed on Ireland.

The second strand revealed a Celtic form of Christianity. The Celts came from Galatia,[3] among other places, and many researchers believe that the stream of Christianity emanating from Ephesus flowed through the Celtic migrants up through Gaul and into Ireland.

These migrating peoples gave Ireland its common language, a common code of law, a common tradition of oral poetry and music and a common history, which was in stark contrast to the prevailing mood of warring tribalism. All this has helped to shape what we see today as Irish culture and identity. Unfortunately through the centuries when English government forces imposed their will on Ireland, they also imposed first a Roman (in the twelfth century) and second a Protestant Christianity (in the sixteenth century) on its people. They also sought to eradicate its culture and language, as well as its prevailing form of spirituality – be it pagan, Celtic Christianity, or Roman Catholicism.

At the same time English government policy attempted to subdue the warring factions (of Irish and English origins!) in order to create a common unity – something that is still elusive in the political, territorial and religious tribalism that predominates in Northern Ireland.

The imposition of belief has been perceived as not only coming from a 'superior' form of Christianity, but also consistently from a superior neighbour – England. Therein lies the problem!

Twelfth Century –
Anglo-Norman Conquest of Ireland

'Although the conquest involved negotiation and alliance as well as warfare, the Anglo-Normans were among the most formidable warriors in Europe, and the Irish were not inclined to submit meekly, so blood shed in the pursuit of power, soaked the foundations of political relationships between England and Ireland.

'From the beginning of their presence in Ireland, the Anglo-Normans condemned Irish culture, so different from their own, as barbarous, with the effect that their efforts to subdue Ireland were justified in their own minds as a civilising and Christianising mission.'[4]

The Anglo-Norman Conquest of Ireland in 1170 AD

followed the granting to Henry II of England of the over-lordship of Ireland by the then pope. Pope Adrian wanted Henry his cousin to bring Ireland into the Catholic faith. As elsewhere, this led to a form of State–Church relationship that has been with us ever since. It was from this time, more particularly, that the imposition of political will was coupled with religious belief and practice.

The imposition of religious beliefs by force has been a plague on the history of Ireland – whether it was a Catholic form or a later Protestant one. The fruit of this is seen in the present-day antagonism between Catholic South and Protestant North – a conflict which is a mere 450 years old, but was rooted here much earlier!

Sixteenth Century – Imposition of Reformation

After the Reformation which followed Henry VIII's secession from the Church of Rome, England entered a bloody era, when 'Protestantism' was enforced on its subjects. The Catholic Church, using friendly European powers, was intent on bringing down Protestant Britain – by almost any means available. Hence Catholic Ireland became a serious threat to our national security. In Ireland the Reformation began in 1536 and combined religious, political and economic interests in a close bond. These interests, as we have seen elsewhere in Britain's colonies, became visibly and tightly entwined at many points in Irish history. For years there was resistance, resulting in rebellion, numerous battles and consequent loss of life.

Because the imposition of Protestantism was so closely tied to the State, resistance by Catholics was interpreted as rebellion against the State – and to some extent it was. The native Irish did not wish their country to continue as a province of England, but wanted it to be a self-governing nation. The whole sorry process included enforced settlement of Protestants from Scotland and England, who systematically took over land from the 'rebellious' Irish after it had been confiscated by Government forces. The religious element of the Reformation had failed to make much progress in Ireland so the English Government employed force to impose it. The ancient tribal spirit of

Ulster was always, it appears, difficult to subdue. The only way the English could handle it was to bring 'plantation'. A 'controlling spirit' in Northern Ireland seems to persist, whoever has been in power.

'Protestant prosperity was built on the unjust foundation of Catholic dispossession. The story of the English crown in Ireland is understood as the story of Irish dispossession, and the colonisation of Ulster is perhaps the central symbol of that story. Plantation gave new vigour and impetus to a process that would eventually see Irish Catholics reduced to an almost landless community.'[5]

By 1714 only 7 per cent of Irish land was owned by Catholics, and they had access only to the poorest land available, effectively imposing poverty on the Catholic native Irish.

'After the Reformation, the traditional English-equals-civilised, Irish-equals-barbarian equations remained as before. But the Reformation also provided a new twist to the 'barbarism' legacy by transmuting it into the terms of conflict between Protestant and Catholic. For centuries many an anti-Catholic sermon spoke in the idiom of barbarism, and it does not require an especially sensitive ear to catch continuing resonances.'[6]

Still today the insensitive, aggressive, intimidating language of some Protestant leaders from the North of Ireland is difficult for Christians elsewhere in the world to stomach. We feel shame and sorrow at some of the un-Christlike assertions made by those with whom we might share a common faith.

Seventeenth Century – Sieges and Bloodshed

Four dates in this period are engraved on the minds of modern-day Irish people:

- 1641, when the Gaelic Irish Catholics rebelled against their Protestant and British overlords;
- 1649, when Protestant Cromwell's invading forces massacred Catholics in Drogheda and Wexford;
- 1689, when the siege of Derry occurred; and

– 1690, when the Dutch William of Orange defeated James II in the Battle of the Boyne.

The atrocities committed by both sides during this period were appalling. People were buried alive, women and children were thrown into the river to drown or be shot, others were tortured and scourged, then left to die. Cromwell had been leader of the Roundheads in the English Civil War to overthrow Charles I, and with him the monarchy. He was also intent on imposing Protestantism where it had not yet taken root. In Ireland there were strong Royalist armies in league with Irish Catholic rebels. In 1649 Cromwell came over and ruthlessly put down the Catholics. He viewed himself as accomplishing God's work by avenging the atrocities of the 1641 rebellion. But unfortunately Drogheda – the site of the massacre – did not feature in the 1641 rebellion. He was actually putting to the sword English Catholics and Royalists – not only Irish ones! Among the horrors of Cromwell's invasion, people taking refuge in a church were slaughtered, Catholic landowners were dispossessed by his Protestant Puritan army, and soldiers taken prisoner were shipped to the New World colonies of America. Altogether, between 1641 and 1652, 112,000 people of English extraction, and 504,000 Irish, died from sword, plague or famine.

Cromwell defended his actions as 'godly vengeance for Catholic massacres of Protestants'. 'All this was done by the Spirit of God', he wrote,[7] so imparting a religious dimension to these events that has persisted through the subsequent three hundred and fifty years. Cromwell's massacres have become 'a key component in the communal memory of domination and victimization', reinforcing Irish perception of 'genocidal intentions by the English in Ireland'.[8]

In a similar way the uprising by Catholics has produced fear and suspicion among Protestants reinforcing a long-held belief that Catholics cannot be trusted, that the nature of Catholicism inevitably yields barbarous acts and that therefore Protestants must always be vigilant lest similar uprisings occur. Both sides have come to view themselves as a people under siege.

Eighteenth and Nineteenth Century – Penal Laws and Potato Famine

The imposition of Penal Laws by the Irish Parliament from 1695 ensured that native Irish Catholics would always be poor. They were discriminated against by the law by reason of their religion (Catholic) or their ethnic origin (Irish). The intention was to cow into submission to the Crown all Irish and by coercion to make them all Protestants. The laws were directed against Catholic religion, land and political power. But the English didn't succeed. The sense of injustice and persecution ensured the survival of both Catholics and Irish. Some worked the system in order to stay alive, others formed secret societies in order to undermine it.

But even more injustice was to come in addition to the massacres and the Penal Laws. 'No event in Irish history has had a more emotional effect on Irish national feeling than the Great Famine of 1845–9. It is not infrequently thought that it was a form of genocide engineered by the English against the Irish people.'[9]

During these years, failure of the potato crop precipitated a horrible famine, resulting in one million deaths from starvation, malnutrition and disease, and the emigration (some of it enforced) of another 1.6 million people. Famine victims were almost exclusively poor Catholics. Because the reaction of the British Parliament was totally inadequate and downright unjust and callous, 'The famine, remembered as an exceptionally brutal example of British colonization, has been the source of exceptional anger.'[10]

Despite being denied basic human rights, Irish Catholics have survived and have continued to make a major contribution to the missionary endeavour of Catholicism worldwide. Similarly Northern Irish Protestants have survived and have made a major contribution to Protestant missionary endeavour worldwide. We believe that one of the redemptive gifts of the Irish to the world is to be a missionary nation. The enemy of souls has sought to rob them of this potential by reinforcing their divisions and ancient hatreds. The Irish were some of the first to bring the gospel to the rest of the

British Isles. So we need to be grateful to God and to them for this great gift.

Twentieth Century – Looking for Solutions

At the beginning of this century, during his term as Prime Minister, Asquith introduced legislation that would have given Home Rule to Ireland and would effectively have made Ireland independent from England for the first time for centuries. But the Protestants rebelled against this, taking the slogan, 'Home Rule Means Rome Rule'. All the ancient antagonisms and fears came to the surface: all that their forefathers had died for was at risk. Protestants were actually afraid of losing their religious and civil liberties at this time. They feared that as a minority in the whole of Ireland, they would be discriminated against, and more importantly, that their Protestant Reformed faith would be at risk in a united Catholic Ireland. They still adhered to the Christendom ideal of the Christian one-faith state – just like the Catholics.

In 1912 an estimated 80 per cent of all Protestant men signed the Ulster Covenant, many in their own blood. They formed the Ulster Volunteer Force (one of the most violent of the para-military groups), and legally resisted the elected government – all of these were actions that could hardly be defended from Scripture. Then in 1921 partition occurred, with the Irish Free State (later to be the Republic of Ireland) and Northern Ireland being given their own separate governments. The rest, as they say, is history. Hard-line Republicans, intent on securing a United Ireland, have pursued their campaign resulting in armed revolt, civil war, terrorism and bloodshed. Once more, different communities have been under siege and have suffered injustices, intimidation, ethnic cleansing and violence – all in the name of Christianity in either a Catholic or Protestant guise!

Over the years there have been many prayer vigils at some of the historic sites, prayer walks around some of the battered towns, and prayer gatherings between Protestants and Catholics. But still the bitterness, hatred, fear and sectarianism have persisted. In 1995 and again in 1998 sixty intercessors gathered to pray for Ireland. Two-thirds were Protestant and one-third Catholic. Some were direct descendants of the early

Scottish Protestant settlers, or of native Irish victims of land
robbery. Others represented those Irish who had been
banished to other countries. Some had come from England
to face up to their country's woeful catalogue of offences
against the Irish. For two days, there was much weeping
before God and confession before one another as we all
sought to take responsibility for the corporate sins of our
respective groups in the past.

Since then opportunity has been given, through some
divine appointments, to try and deal with the legacy of the
past at national level. In December 1994 the Archbishop of
Canterbury publicly apologised in Dublin Cathedral for what
the English had done to the Irish. In February 1995 the
Roman Catholic Primate of all Ireland apologised in Canterbury Cathedral for what the Irish had done to the English.
Such acts and statements can only be positive in helping to
heal the wounds of the past. We need to pray for the process
to continue at all levels of society. We as English need to
apologise again and again to Irish Catholics and Northern
Irish Protestants for the way the sins of England have
offended, damaged and alienated their forebears. We need
to show to both groups that we love and accept them, and
ask them to accept and forgive us.

Wales

As we have seen so often elsewhere, the history of
Welsh/English relationships has been of the numerically
superior English overrunning the smaller Welsh nation.
Originally independent Wales was conquered by Edward I
of England and united with England by the Statute of Wales
in 1284. Since 1301 the title 'Prince of Wales' has been
conveyed on the eldest son of the reigning monarch. Wales
is a land of castles – none more famous than Caernarfon,
ancient home of past kings of Wales. So, when the Prince
of Wales was 'invested' with his title in a ceremony at
Caernarfon castle, all the ancient antagonisms were stirred.

Although not as bitter nor as violent nor as prolonged
historically as in the case of Ireland, opposition and suspicion are still present. Even in Christian circles when

evangelistic or other events are organised, it is usually the English – in name or in speech – who do the planning, take the leadership, and run things their way. They are motivated by their desire to see the kingdom of God extended in Wales and many have come as the result of a missionary call, but often they are perceived as doing the 'English' thing and calling the shots, and the Welsh themselves feel marginalised. Their sense of inferiority – the product of events of history – is reinforced.

A friend has recently returned from holiday in Wales. 'In some villages they still spit on the ground after an Englishman has walked past', she told me. Many from England who buy country cottages in Wales as an investment or as a holiday home, have had their homes burned to the ground by 'Welsh extremists'. Promoters of the Welsh language have frequently accused the English of trying to rob the Welsh of their culture. Once again, we see a similar pattern of antagonism emerging.

What has England done in the past that has given rise to this antagonism? It has subjugated a nation, sought to take away its identity and its culture, and even to ignore its language with the result that seven hundred years later, the Welsh still feel a deep hostility towards the English.

An Historic Overview

After the departure of the Romans, around 400 AD, there followed two hundred years of completely different history and experience for the people left behind in Wales to those in other parts of Britain. The Romans had never allowed civilians to carry arms, and so the 'civilised' people of Eastern and Central Britain, with no training in the use of weapons or tactics for war, were an easy prey for the land-hungry Jutes, Angles and Saxons, all hailing from Germany. They came first as raiders then as settlers, driving out or killing all who opposed them. They initially settled in present-day South, East and North-east England. During these 'Dark Ages' the whole of what is now England was thoroughly Saxonised, as these invaders successfully established their culture, religion, legends, myths, and language, as well as their own methods of farming, house building and village community life.

In Wales the situation was different. They had never abandoned their martial skills, so were largely able to repel invaders, and during these years the country as a whole enjoyed a period known as 'The Age of Saints' or 'The Age of Light'. Missionaries sailed up the Western seas from Brittany and Ireland, settled in Wales, founded innumerable Christian communities and were successful in converting the poorest country people as well as their various rulers. By the year 597 AD when Augustine was sent from Rome to convert the pagan Saxons of England, the Saxons were loathed, feared and scorned by the Welsh Celtic Christians, who unfortunately had no desire at all to see them saved. Augustine's total lack of sensitivity to the situation, and his overbearing manner and behaviour, alienated even further the leaders of the Welsh Church, as he also had the Celtic bishops from elsewhere in Britain.

This feeling of isolationism was more than strengthened during the next four hundred years leading up to the Norman conquest of England. Although some Welsh rulers made alliances with Christian Saxon kings such as Alfred and his immediate successors, there were continual defensive wars and raids against the Mercians on the other side of Offa's dyke.[11] During this period there was a great deal of in-fighting and minor wars between the many local chieftains, princes and rulers, punctuated by periods of relative peace when one strong man dominated the scene. The common people only enjoyed peace when a really strong, forceful character came into power and subdued all other contestants. But whereas in England, people were assimilating the rich variety of thought and culture brought in by the Danes, the Norsemen, and travellers from across the English Channel, in Wales the determination to resist rather than assimilate was strengthened and the country became increasingly isolated and inward-looking.

The date 1066 is imprinted on the memory of most English people as the true beginning of their history as a nation. The Norman Conquest was sudden and complete, with the virtual elimination of the Saxon lords at the Battle of

Hastings. William himself was a blood relative of the last Saxon king, and as such was more easily accepted by the people. Most of those who came with him from France were landless younger sons who had no intention of returning home when there was now the opportunity of stepping into a dead Saxon's shoes and taking up his role as lord of the manor. The Saxon people needed leaders and the Norman adventurers needed a proletariat, and so it was in their interests to come to terms with each other. Two generations later, after a good deal of intermarriage and integration, we hear of people of both sides equally proud to call themselves 'Englishmen'. The feudal system had been firmly established throughout the land, but the old Common Law was retained and respected and gradually they all began to speak one language.

History shows us a different picture in Wales, where Norman infiltration was limited to the border country, a few scattered royal fortresses, the fertile plains of the Severn and Wye valleys and along the southern coast. Wherever the Normans gained a foothold they built a castle and, in true colonial style, brought in English settlers to establish a town, raise a defensive wall, and make a profitable living servicing the needs of the castle dwellers. They looked down their noses at the native Welsh in the hills around them, who lived such a different lifestyle. The native people of Wales were still true Celts in culture, thought and lifestyle. And, of course, they spoke an entirely different language. The hostility and suspicion must have been mutual.

The real turning-point in Welsh history came in 1282 with the betrayal and death of their last great leader, Llewelyn, who only fifteen years earlier had received the homage of all the other Welsh princes and had been recognised as Prince of all Wales by the ageing Henry III. No doubt seeing this new unity as a threat to his sovereignty, Edward I, with vastly superior military technology and almost unlimited wealth and resources, carefully planned and successfully carried out a three-pronged invasion and ultimate conquest of the whole country of Wales. For the first time after such an invasion he granted no amnesty to those who sought mercy, and jailed or executed all the leaders who had fought against him. Then he set about stamping out the independence and Welshness of the Welsh with ferocious determination, reorganising the country into English shires, introducing English law in the courts, installing his own sheriffs and justiciaries, and insisting on the English language being the only one used in settling disputes. In spite of this, due in part to the geography of the country, many rural parts of Wales remained virtually unanglicised well into the twentieth century. (In Merioneth in the 1940s some teenage schoolchildren were failed in a musical examination because they were unable to speak or understand English.) In any case, when one considers that there were at least thirteen centuries of continuous Celtic background and inheritance, and only seven centuries between that and the present day, it is not surprising that many of the ways of thinking and characteristics of the two peoples remain very different.

The Legacy of Oppression in Wales

Eleventh Century

When William of Normandy settled Marcher Barons along the borders of Wales, he gave them full permission to increase the size of their holdings by taking as much land as they could from the Welsh. They were allowed to make and administer their own laws and became virtually an all-powerful law unto themselves. The native people were driven out of the fertile cattle and arable country of the valleys and plains up into the rocky, sour and marshy land of the hill country, and when they brought a raiding party down to recapture some of their stolen property, they were branded as 'hill robbers' and 'cattle thieves'.

Twelfth Century

The simplicity and spirituality of the Celtic Church was scorned and despised and the unwritten, oral traditions of a place or community were swept aside when the Normans moved in, so that when a castle was built and a town established, the local church was also rebuilt (often with a defensive stone tower) and rededicated to St Mary, St Michael, or possibly St Andrew – obviously more acceptable to the new men of power than St Stinian, St Curig or St Teilo.

Fourteenth Century

After the uprising of Madoc in 1294, Welshmen and women were no longer permitted to live within the walls of a town amongst the English settlers, but were driven out into the surrounding countryside. This might not have been such a hardship, except that all artisans, tradesmen and people of any standing at all were by the same law required to reside within the walls, and thus people of Welsh descent were forced to pursue the only livelihoods remaining, namely as hill shepherds or mercenary bowmen in the King's foreign wars. The policy seems to have been to make and keep the Welsh poor, and then despise them for their poverty.

Fifteenth Century

Following the rising of Owain Glyndwr a century later, oppression and cruelty increased, but one is given to understand that many of the vindictive laws passed at that time were not always enforced. Wales was inevitably drawn into the fighting and bitterness of the Wars of the Roses (1455–85): both Edward IV and Richard III were from the house of Mortimer (Earls of March on the Brecon border), and one of the chief protagonists of the house of Lancaster was Earl of Pembroke. There was much bloodshed, recriminations and changing of sides.

Sixteenth Century

The advent of the Tudors brought only disappointment for the people of Wales. Henry VII, who landed in Pembrokeshire from France in 1485, was of Welsh descent on his father's side, and from Edward III on his mother's. Born in Pembroke Castle, he had never lived in England, and, from his exile in France, had promised to do great things for the Welsh people if he became king. Most of these promises never materialised and the high hopes of the Welsh turned sour. On his death, matters became worse when his son Henry VIII introduced oppressive laws: not only did it become illegal to speak the Welsh language but the final culmination was the Act of Union of 1536, which some historians see as the worst thing that could have happened to Wales as a country. 'The brave vigorous, confident people of the middle ages ... were replaced by servile and undignified people who believed that it was their duty and their privilege to enrich and strengthen England.'[12]

Eighteenth Century

The Church became very run down during this period, being ruled by absentee bishops who sometimes only visited their diocese once a year. English vicars were appointed to parishes where only Welsh was spoken and were unable to communicate with their parishioners. Doubtless, this contributed to the resentment and bitterness felt during what has been called the Tithe Wars. With the rise of Methodism and the Dissenters – indeed, the whole non-conformist Church – many were converted anew to Christianity and started attending one of the specially built chapels, committing themselves to the support of a minister or pastor who actually shared their language and beliefs. They were still legally obliged to support the Anglican incumbent with the payment of tithes, and there are reports of bailiffs being sent in to seize a poor family's one and only cow, or even the bed beneath the dying body of a poor grandfather. Naturally, some of these injustices were resisted.

Nineteenth Century

The effects of the Industrial Revolution which had started in England were different in Wales, where the whole process was much more sudden and hurried. Deep divisions in Welsh society increased and now included a rift between the rural and industrial communities, heightening the tension between North and South. The anglicised gentry and their Welsh tenants were miles apart in thought and culture (a middle class hardly existed), and the rift was deepening. With the coming of the vote, matters really came to a head. The ballot was open and landlords began to turn out from their farms any tenants who voted against them and, where eviction took place, no compensation could be claimed. This began in Merioneth in 1859, but spread to Caernarfon, Cardigan and Carmarthen. Some evictions were also made on religious grounds, where tenants refused to attend the local Anglican church. It was not until 1893 that Gladstone set up a Commission of Enquiry which completely vindicated the tenant farmer.

Twentieth Century

It is due to the grace of God that at the beginning of the twentieth century, Wales should receive a visitation of the Holy Spirit through the Welsh Revival. Born in an atmosphere of prayer and spontaneous singing, the revival touched many parts of Wales. However, it was the native Welsh speaking – the downtrodden – whom God particularly touched. Until criticism and influence from some English leaders seemed to cut off the flow!

The effects of the short-lived revival were felt like ripples (or shock waves) all around the world. Wales became a blessing to the nations. Recently some intercessory leaders in Wales have caught deeply in their spirits the fact that God wants to restore to them what was cut off in the revival. They are ready once more to become a blessing to the nations. It is imperative, therefore, that the English, through humbling ourselves and repenting of our intimidating and oppressive ways, help to pave the way for God to use the Welsh once more.

What needs to be done by way of reconciliation towards the Welsh? We need to apologise for our collective cultural and linguistic arrogance and superiority, and for the ways over the centuries in which they have been marginalised economically, socially and politically. This has been a marginalisation on both a Christian/spiritual level, and on an English/Welsh one. Whatever we as English people attempt to contribute in Wales – even evangelism – if we come across as having a superior attitude, it will inevitably result in alienation. So we as Christians cannot ignore this issue. We need to take responsibility for all the atrocities and injustices committed over many centuries.

Our contention is that the deeply ingrained prejudices of many centuries cannot be ignored or dismissed light-heartedly. They affect the attitudes of sincere, spiritually-minded leaders and their ability to welcome and receive from their English counterparts. Some still feel inferior and alienated because of this history. If that is the case amongst Christians, how much more is it so among the rest of the population? Therefore English Christian leaders must begin to acknowledge the sins of their forebears in order to bring some healing into these relationships, and to prepare for future co-operation in making Christ known, and opening up again the wells of blessing!

Scotland

Scotland as a nation, with its own cultural history and development, did not come into being until 844 AD. Prior to that it was one with the rest of Britain. The early Christian heritage in Scotland had a Roman source, with Ninian, a Briton trained in Rome, evangelising the Picts in the fifth century. The Picts may have been the original inhabitors of the northern areas of present-day Scotland. However, Gaelic-speaking migrants from Ireland, who were called 'Scots', gave Scotland its name. Christianity in its monastic form first came to Scotland from Ireland too. Iona and Whithorn were among the earliest places to be settled by St Columba in 563 AD. At this time the missionary endeavour of travelling monks from Ireland spread the gospel into many parts of Europe.

This common history with Ireland has meant that there is little evidence of antagonism between Ireland and Scotland, despite the fact that during the sixteenth-century plantation of Ireland, Scottish farmers were the ones being resettled, bringing with them a Calvinistic form of Presbyterianism – indeed, half of those who were encouraged to settle in Ireland by the British Government of the time were Scottish. So today, in Ireland as in Scotland, the strongest Protestant denomination is the Presbyterian Church. Yet strangely, although Protestantism in its Presbyterian form is strongly resisted by Catholic Ireland (and vice-versa), the Scottish connection has not attracted the same antagonism.

The Reformation was particularly strong in Scotland. As we have already mentioned, because the Roman Empire did not succeed in establishing itself in Scotland, the Roman Church never became as strong there as it did in England. The Reformation brought to England an Anglican expression of Christianity with its Church/State emphasis, instead of the former Roman one. However, in Scotland, it was a different

expression that took root. Calvinism, with its strong theological emphasis, produced Scottish Presbyterianism. So by
the mid-sixteenth century, Scotland had become Presbyterian, whilst England and the English crown were Anglican.
This was partly due to political reasons: Mary Queen of
Scots was married to the King of France, a country which
was England's enemy and Catholic, so it was in England's
interests to allow Presbyterianism to flourish!

However, the suspicion and antagonism towards England
that exists in Scotland is not so tied in with religious history as
it is with political and tribal causes. Scots talk of their history
in terms of defeats by the English on the battlefields. That is
why rivalry on today's football and rugby fields is seen as an
opportunity to parade and indulge national pride. The so-
called 'tartan army' is seen as menacing whenever it 'invades'
England. It is the joy of every nation to defeat the English!

It is this history of defeat and an inability to trust the
English that have caused Scotland to be suspicious towards
anything English. Even today new facets of Christian belief
are less likely to take root in Scotland if they have first
emerged and flourished in England. New Christian initiatives
are not likely to succeed either, unless they have been started
by the Scots themselves. Some would say that this is indicat-
ive of a more theologically conservative Scottish outlook,
whereas others see this rather as a reflection of Scottish
nationalism or of resistance to the English, or both.

Why is this so? Is it important for us to do anything about
it? Yes it is, particularly if it is a perception that affects
people's openness to the gospel and to the unity between
those with a common allegiance to Jesus Christ.

In recent years there has been a resurgence of Scottish
national pride. This has been fed by films like *Braveheart*,
Robert the Bruce, *Chasing the Deer*, and *The Highland Clearances*. English families living in Scotland have begun to face
discrimination and intimidation. Scottish identity and pride
have also been encouraged by a spate of new Scottish folk
songs, the persuasive politics of the Scottish Nationalist Party
and its proposals for economic and political devolution
leading to independence! The ancient antagonisms are being
stirred.

Why is this anti-English feeling, coupled with a desire to separate from English rule, so strong? Again, history holds the answer. For over seven hundred years that legacy of mistrust and, at times, hatred has existed between England and Scotland. There are deep injustices in the past that have to be resolved in order for the destructive forces to be counteracted. Untreated wounds do not heal themselves.

From 1292 King Edward I of England began to impose English rule on Scotland. From then on there were sporadic engagements and battles for more than two hundred years. Each time England won, they went 'over the top' in unjustified slaughter. In 1296 Edward invaded Scotland. On Good Friday he sacked the undefended town of Berwick – at that time the largest and most prosperous in Scotland. **Seventeen thousand** inhabitants were butchered and their bodies left to rot in the streets. As 90 per cent of Scotland's wealth was owned by Berwick, and most of the trade was handled from there, he also plunged Scotland into two hundred years of poverty. From there his vastly superior army defeated a small Scottish army at Dunbar. Not content with this, he later forced the remaining Scottish aristocracy, clan chiefs and churchmen in a mass act of allegiance to swear fealty to him in 'stinking Berwick' – the city of the 'rotting dead'. The Stone of Destiny, upon which Scottish monarchs had always been invested with their royal authority, was taken south and placed in Westminster Abbey. It was returned to Scotland in 1997, seven hundred years later. Commenting about the sacking of Berwick, Janet R. Glover wrote:

> 'By this one preliminary action, Edward implanted that bitter hatred for all things English which was to be nourished so consistently by English policy during the next three hundred years.'[13]

As Edward died in 1307, he cursed Scotland across the Solway Firth from Burgh on Sands. Berwick was to change hands thirteen times – seldom without bloodshed.

Two centuries later in 1513 at the battle of Flodden Field, not far from Berwick, James IV of Scotland was killed along with bishops, earls and thousands of Scotland's nobility and young men – the cream of Scottish youth – by the smaller but better trained English force. Henry VIII had joined most of Europe in an alliance against France. Most unwisely James IV had responded to a French plea for assistance by attacking the North of England with a huge army of over 60,000 men. James even sent the veteran Earl of Surrey, who had been left in charge in England, notice that he was coming. It ended in the horror of the greatest military defeat Scotland has ever suffered. Again towns, villages, monasteries and farmlands were wrecked. Again a whole generation of Scottish males were annihilated. Two hundred years of English/Scottish conflict left another legacy of hatred and hostility that survives to this day. Not satisfied with victory in battle, English raiding parties continued to penetrate deep into Scotland for another year, on an orgy of killing, raping, burning, robbery and vengeance. Defenceless, the people cowered.

Henry VIII, instigator of the Reformation in England, demanded the marriage of the baby Queen Mary to his son, Edward VI. When the Scots refused, he invaded Scotland in 1544, sacking Leith as Berwick had been sacked 250 years earlier. He also ruined 243 villages, 5 market towns and the border abbeys. Raids once again continued – until 1547. 'The cruelties of the English in these campaigns did ineradicable harm ... worse still was the legacy of hatred.'[14]

More conflict occurred in the Cromwellian period – firstly in the battle of Philiphaugh near Selkirk. In 1638 the Scottish Presbyterians signed a National Covenant, largely as a re-action to the imposition of English Episcopalianism on their country. They swore to take up arms to defend the liberty of their Kirk. Charles I sent an army north to impose his will. But neither side wanted a conflict, so a treaty was drawn up at Berwick. However, when civil war broke out in England in 1642, the Scottish Covenanters sided with Cromwell against the Royalists – at least initially. Later Montrose, one of the Covenanters, changed sides. He met his first defeat at Philiphaugh against 6000 Covenanters. After the battle, the prisoners and wounded were massacred, followed by women and children. 'All who were caught were slain without pity, and all in the name of religion. For it was done to the glory of

God, the excesses urged on by the blood-crazed Covenanting ministers of the kirk.' [15]

In 1650 Cromwell marched north to try to subdue Scotland. He defeated the Covenanter army near Dunbar. The same extreme Covenant divines who had demanded the slaughter of the Royalist prisoners now gave the command to go down and smite Cromwell. This was now a Protestant against Protestant conflict, interpreted because of the history, as an Anglo/Scottish issue. Neither was that the end. In 1683 the Government under Charles II ordered the emptying of the gaols of adulterers, murderers and thieves in order to accommodate those against whom theological charges could be made! How can we face the horror of Church-sanctioned slaughter being meted out against those of a different view? It is unjustifiable.

The eventual result of this was the enforcing of the Act of Union on Scotland in 1707, but not before many other losses and much treachery! In 1698 William Patterson, a founder of the Bank of England, formed a trading fleet, with 1200 colonists to establish a colony in Panama. No English were allowed to participate in this venture. This whole expedition was killed in action with the Spanish or through disease. Two other expeditions followed, with the same result. Scotland had subscribed nearly a third of her resources and, along with all the personnel, every penny was lost. This brought home to the Scots that they needed the English if they were to develop their material wellbeing and survive economically. So they sought for an Act of Union. But the English endeavoured to squeeze the best deal for themselves out of this. They passed an act in Parliament which threatened a blockade against all trade, and declared that all Scots living in England would be classed as aliens. The Scottish landowners backed the deal, having been suitably bribed by the English Government. But the majority of the population was against it. Immediately the terms were broken and resented. The whole country rose in uproar and outrage. Pro-union sympathisers were in danger of their lives.

The ensuing taxation against the Scots ensured that they would never be able to trade on equal terms with England or her trading partners. This simmering discontent indirectly led to the Scots' support of the Old Pretender (Catholic James VIII) and the uprising of 1715.

The same discontent surfaced again and led to support for the Young Pretender, which eventually resulted in the Battle of Culloden in 1745. Bonnie Prince Charlie put together an expeditionary force with the help of Jacobites. Again there was a French connection. They were ostensibly helping Louis XV by creating a diversion in England, but it was doomed to failure. They marched on London with the aim of declaring Charles the Pretender as king. Alas they aborted the campaign and returned to Scotland without reaching London. Meanwhile troops returning from Flanders under the leadership of the Duke of Cumberland were deployed against the Scots. Well-armed and experienced, they caught the Jacobites near Culloden, east of Inverness. Charles' army was already exhausted by lack of food and forced marches, and they suffered a devastating defeat.

Yet again an English army went beyond what was required in a blood lust. All stragglers were ordered to be killed and no mercy was to be shown, even to the wounded. 'The Duke organised a systematic burning of homes, including remote hovels. He had thousands of cattle rounded up for confiscation. The disaster he inflicted on the Highlands caused terrible destitution.' [16] The Government executed 120 people from the Jacobite movement, so wiping it out. Eleven hundred were exiled and 700 died in gaols. Bagpipes were confiscated along with weapons and the wearing of tartan was forbidden.

Nothing was more designed to humiliate the Scots than this. Although it was perceived as an English versus Scots battle, and a Catholic versus Protestant one, the truth is different. There were Catholics and Protestants on both sides. Clans fought each other on both sides. It was possibly London Government versus the rest.

The outcome of all this was the passing of harsh laws in order to subdue the spirit of the highlanders and give the English 'an habitual superiority'. No wonder the Scots still harbour a hatred for all things English and a desire to be free of what some still see as a yoke of oppression and a continuing subjugation of a nation.

Again the remedy for these conflicts, for the continued hatred and antagonism and for the arrogance is found at the cross. There our hostility was nailed (Ephesians 2:16), and there reconciliation is made real – both with God and with one another.

In the past five years we have been involved in Prayer Conferences at the sites of some of the important events in Scottish history, the last of which was at Flodden Field and at Berwick. We have found a number of times how a simple public apology, deeply felt and genuinely expressed, has defused antagonism, removed hatred and brought healing. Scots have come to us and said in effect, 'I didn't realise how much hatred I had for the English until you apologised. God used that to take the hatred away and change my attitude.' If this can be true among Christians, how much more hatred persists among the non-Christian population? And what will God do in them when they hear and see genuine contrition for past corporate sin? Confession is powerful, contrition is compelling, and reconciliation then flows to remove barriers to our personal and corporate walk with God. Yet confession is at its most effective when we are able to get right back to the roots of these deep wounds.

Notes

1. Sir Fred Catherwood, *Pro Europe?* (IVP, 1991), pp. 35, 47.
2. Joseph Liechty, 'Roots of Sectarianism in Ireland', p. 4 – a paper commissioned for a Working Party on Sectarianism set up by the Department of Social Issues of the Irish Inter-Church Meeting.
3. In modern-day Turkey, in the vicinity of Ankara.
4. Liechty, 'Roots of Sectarianism in Ireland'. pp. 3, 4.
5. Ibid., p. 10.
6. Ibid., pp. 4, 5.
7. Robert Kee, *Ireland a History* (Abacus, 1995).
8. Liechty, 'Roots of Sectarianism in Ireland'.
9. Kee, *Ireland a History*, p. 77.
10. Liechty, 'Roots of Sectarianism in Ireland'.
11. The Normans (or Norsemen) originally came from Scandinavia, but had inhabited northern France (now Normandy). The Mercians, descendants of the Angles, were border men living around Wessex, Northumbria and Wales.
12. Gwynfor Evans, *Land of my Fathers: 2000 Years of Welsh History* (J. Penry P., 1974), p. 282.

13. *The Story of Scotland* (Faber, 1960), p. 66.
14. Ibid., p. 111.
15. Nigel Tranter, *The Illustrated Portrait of the Border Country* (Hale, 1987), p. 135.
16. Janet Glover, *The Story of Scotland*, p. 179.

Chapter 15

What Shall We Do?

Finding Root Causes

In Revelation 2 the apostle John exhorts the Ephesian church to return to its first love. Losing your spiritual roots is to church what losing your compass bearing is to a vessel: at best dangerous and at worst disastrous. John gives the Ephesians the choice of repenting or losing their lampstand. The latter would presumably mean losing the Spirit of Jesus and ceasing to be true church at all.

The spiritual roots of the British Church lie in part in centuries past in the Christianity of Patrick, the apostle. He was born into a 'Christian' family, his father being a Roman state official and a church deacon. As a youngster he was kidnapped from Scotland and taken to Ireland where he found Christ in a personal way. Escaping to France, he was discipled by Christians of the Johannine tradition (flowing out of Ephesus interestingly enough) and then returned as a missionary to Ireland. It was from there that the gospel spread out first throughout the Celtic areas of Wales and Scotland and finally to England.

It is no coincidence that there is such a renewal of interest in Celtic Christianity today. It has great prophetic significance: God is speaking to the British Church and calling us back to our first love. The fact that this interest is also in the secular sphere only confirms that it is sufficiently important to impact society widely. God is speaking to us.

The question that has concerned us throughout the whole process of revelation and research we attempt to describe in this book is the question of roots. Where did the root of oppression and bitterness get into our national history? The writer to the Hebrews challenges us to so lead *'that no root of bitterness springing up causes trouble and by it many be defiled'* (Hebrews 12:15). This is clearly a crucial question.

In September 1995 I took a week to fast, pray and seek God for an answer, among other things, to this question. About that time I had received a copy of Michael Mitton's book *Restoring the Woven Cord: Strands of Celtic Christianity for Today's Church.*[1] Whilst reading it I was impressed with the possibility that the answer might lie in Bede's *Ecclesiastical History of the English People* completed in 731 AD. This book clearly carries important ancient material. I resolved to get hold of a modern English version as soon as possible. Within a week I was in Omaha, Nebraska, USA. To my surprise and amazement my host asked me innocently on my second day there whether I was interested in church history. When I said yes he presented me with a copy of Bede in modern English. I felt that we were onto something. I burnt the midnight oil that night and found what I believe is important root material. This is not new to many of course, but I believe that the Lord introduced me to it in this way because He wanted to underline its importance.

The incident relates to the encounter between the two streams of Christianity, the Roman which was represented by Augustine and the Celtic which was represented by the Celtic bishops, who met in 603 to come to an agreement about the evangelisation of England. The key points of the encounter took place, according to Bede, at Augustine's Oak, a place which Christians have attempted to identify precisely and which seems to have been in the vicinity of Cricklade near Swindon, Wiltshire, close to the source of the Thames. (Research and revelation incline me to accept Cricklade, but for the purposes of prophetic intercession absolute exactitude is not vital, it just helps to be as specific and accurate as we can.) The heart of the matter was the unwillingness of the two streams to work together for the evangelisation of the Saxons in mutually supportive brotherhood.

The main fault to begin with was clearly with the Roman delegation. Their desire to work together with the Celtic Church to evangelise the Saxons strategically was laudable but their insistence on the apostolic authority of Rome was narrow-minded and controlling. The Romans' manipulative attitude was made worse by their abuse of spiritual gifts, firstly to insist on compliance and then as a kind of blackmail: Bede describes Augustine's warning that, if the Celts did not submit to his and the Bishop of Rome's authority in evangelising the Saxons, this failure to co-operate would lead to the Celtic Christians being slaughtered by the Saxon armies. Bede described this as a prophecy, I think it was a curse. He goes on to describe its fulfilment a few years later, probably at Chester, when the Celtic king's army was routed at the expense of the deaths of 1200 intercessors who had come from Bangor-on-Dee to pray during the battle.

The Celtic bishops may not have been blameless and were perhaps in danger of identifying the Celtic with the Christian cause at that time. Nevertheless it began a dishonour and rejection of the roots of British Christianity that continued in the development of English Christianity. Seen in this context the sin of England towards Ireland is greatly clarified and is all the worse. The way we forced Roman Catholicism on Ireland with the sword in the twelfth century and then Protestantism at the end of the barrel of a gun in the seventeenth century is seen in an even graver light. It seems that this rejection of true apostolic paternity and inclusiveness by what became the dominant expression of Church in England left its imprint on the development of society as a whole. It became the mark of how England dealt first with its neighbour races of Ireland, Scotland and Wales and in due course its own peasant peoples and much of the rest of the world.

It was with trepidation and not a little awe and excitement that a few friends of mutual respect for the spiritual traditions of both Roman and Celtic forms of Christianity representing different forms of those traditions today and coming from various parts of these islands met in July 1996 at Cricklade to say sorry and attempt the beginnings of ongoing reconciliation ministry on this perhaps the deepest of all wounds in the heart of our nations: the differences and division between Catholics and Protestants, and between Roman and Celtic forms of Christianity. If this could be pursued it would go a long way towards healing the hatred in the hearts of people in many parts of the world. The bitterness and bloodshed, the murders and the martyrdom in the name of Christ over the centuries from both sides have left their mark on Christianity the world over.

The Way Forward

Sin is always wrong. But sin committed by the Church is heinous. Satan points to the sin of the people of God and uses it as ample justification to build strongholds of the same kinds of sins among those who are not godly. Ed Silvoso defines a stronghold as 'a mindset impregnated with hopelessness that causes the believer to accept as unchangeable something that he/she knows is contrary to the will of God.' The Greek word used for 'stronghold' in 2 Corinthians 10:4 literally means 'fortress' or 'castle'. Our habitual sin as the Church makes it possible for Satan to create spiritual strongholds over an area, a people or a nation. And so, vengeful hatred lives on. He goes on and on pursuing his goal of destroying God's creation, committing genocide or infanticide, indulging in ethnic cleansing, or 'avenging' past atrocities. We fail to halt him.

Jesus, an innocent man, was nailed to a cross. Instead of a man who lived a life of love and compassion, humankind chose to save a terrorist and a murderer, and, by so doing, perpetuated a pattern of behaviour that has continued to plague the human race ever since. The innocents are terrorised and more and more righteous blood is shed on the earth. According to a United Nations' report entitled 'The State of the World's Children', nine civilians are killed for every military casualty in modern warfare. Most civilian casualties are women and children – the innocents. Two million children have died in wars in the past ten years.

Countless actions perpetrated over centuries in the name of 'religion' or 'the Church' have given licence to the Enemy to pursue his ruthless goal of destruction. As witness to this, look at Biafra, Bosnia, Cambodia, Rwanda, Ireland and Vietnam. Look at the Holocaust, the Crusades and the various 'holy wars'.

In the days leading up to the crucifixion enemies were reconciled. Herod and Pilate became friends (Luke 23:12) and conspired against Jesus (Acts 4:27). The Jews found they could after all live with the Romans, up until that time their hated adversary, as they insistently demanded that Christ be crucified. Pilate bowed to their vehement calls – the calls of chief priests and leading theologians. Then as now, enemies found common ground in pursuing the innocent and in persecuting the idealists. Then as now, religious leaders sanctioned, and at times conspired in, state violence.

We who are called 'society' release the terrorists and butchers back into the community. We look for rehabilitation of the guilty. We condemn innocent victims to a lifetime of fear. The victimised become the vanquished.

How can the innocent respond to corporate evil on this scale? The next generation takes up arms to gain their revenge. No nation is guiltless, no people fully absolved from the mistakes of their past – all have sinned and fall short of God's glory.

The pattern continues relentlessly until someone calls a stop and does something to break the cycle of violence and bloodshed. This someone was Christ. He died. He thoroughly identified with all the innocents of the world when He became a persecuted minority of one!

Of course, there is only one sacrifice for sins forever and the death of Christ on the cross was fully effective against the enemy. We do not need another crucifixion – Jesus paid the price. But in the same way as we personally appropriate what He did for our personal salvation and for reconciliation with the Father and with one another, we believe it is possible for us to appropriate Christ's sacrificial death to deal with corporate sin – the sin of the Church and the sin of the nation.

Sin has to be confessed and **turned from**. It is no good confessing sin and then turning around and doing the same thing again as if nothing has changed. If, for example, I confess my own sin of racism to a church full of black people, both as a personal statement and as a corporate act on behalf of white people, but then go out and continue to act in a racially motivated way, my confession is worse than useless.

But if my confession turns to repentance and is followed by acts of reconciliation and regard for the rights of the racially different, and if my repentance takes place again and again before different groups, then not only is it effective for me, it is also sowing seeds of acceptance in others and a mood of forgiveness and reconciliation is engendered. It doesn't matter whether I call it repentance or confession, what matters is the fruit.

The question is, can the acknowledgement of corporate sin by one man or woman make any difference? The answer is yes. Look at the confession of Daniel when he acknowledged the guilt, the shame, the misdeeds and the curses caused by the sins of a previous generation (see Daniel 9:1–19). That his prayer was heard and effective we need be in no doubt. That he was not personally implicated we can be sure, because for his own righteousness and unblemished character he was thrust into the lions' den (see Daniel 6:22 where Daniel attributes his deliverance to the fact that he was innocent)!

So here was a righteous man – one man – acknowledging historic sin.

But in general we believe the acknowledgement of such guilt is better when entered into by the Body of Christ, wherever it seems appropriate, but led by those who have felt the anguish of that sin as Daniel (Daniel 9:3), Nehemiah (Nehemiah 1:4) and Ezra did (see Ezra 9:5–7 and 10:1). Just as there has to be conviction of sin by the individual before confession, repentance and reconciliation can follow, so too we need to feel the horror of what has happened in the past. We have to humble ourselves and say 'sorry', both to God and to others.

Certainly where the Church is implicated, the Church needs to take corporate responsibility, with its leaders setting the tone and taking the initiative. When they do, it makes it possible for secular leaders to follow suit. When they refuse to do so or even pretend it doesn't matter, then they give licence to the secular authorities to act in the same way.

In the letters to the seven churches in Revelation 2 and 3, five churches were told to repent corporately. Ephesus had left its first love (half a century after the church was first established). Pergamum had witnessed the violent death of Antipas and held to the teaching of Balaam (stemming back many centuries) in eating idolatrous food and engaging in sexual sin. Thyatira had allowed a Jezebel to take authority, lead people into immorality and teach Satan's secrets. Sardis had lost its reputation and was spiritually dead, and Laodicea had become rich, famous and lethargic. In each case the message was to the church: repent. The command was not to individuals but to the corporate entity of the Church, and along with it came the promise of amazing blessing!

What blessing will God pour out when the Church in Britain starts to deal with its sinful history? None of the seven churches had committed murder nor indulged in such other sin as Britain and the British Church has. But God is still a gracious God who says to us, 'Repent. Humble yourselves.'

When corporate sin is confessed and repented of, the way becomes open for reconciliation. We have frequently seen how, when two individuals confess and ask forgiveness for their wrong words and actions, reconciliation follows. We believe the same happens in a corporate sense.

Imagine what it would be like if the Church not only helped the poor, but also apologised in public for what it has done to make and keep them poor? Or, if our nation apologised to the nations of the former British Empire for past injustices, victimisation and bloodshed, and then offered to do something practical towards making amends (as happened in New Zealand – see chapter 8), thus making it possible for the next generation to recover a sense of destiny and self-worth.

The Church needs to take the lead in all this because the gospel we proclaim is so often rejected. It is rejected not simply because people disbelieve it, but because they see the sins of the so-called Christian nations, and they weigh up the attitudes and actions of our forebears. However well-intentioned the early missionaries were, they were shaped by the sinful attitudes of their own culture, and they and we bear the blame for the things that took place that were wrong in God's eyes. We have mixed blessing with oppressing.

The Christian faith requires confession, repentance and faith. It demands that we prove our repentance by our deeds

(Acts 26:20). That is no less important corporately than it is personally.

When we begin to acknowledge our corporate sin as a Church and own the guilt of our nation, then God will begin to set the stage for the most mighty outpouring of the Holy Spirit both here and in the nations where we are presently hated. He will turn the curses into blessings. The more we bless others, the more blessing will return – that's a biblical principle. God will begin to give prophetic acts to those who 'stand in the gap' at strategic events and times. This will begin to have an effect in breaking the stranglehold of Satan over such nations.

We will be appropriating the sacrifice of Christ for sin.

> *'If we confess our sins* [corporate – our], *He is faithful and righteous to forgive us our sins and to cleanse us from all unrighteousness.'* (1 John 1:9)

We need to remind ourselves that this is written to the believing community: *'My dear children'*. This amazing statement follows:

> *'...He Himself is the propitiation for our sins; and not for ours only, but also for the **sins of the whole world**.'*
> (1 John 2:2, emphasis mine)

Our individualism and individualistic approach to faith and the Word of God have acted as a filter to so much that is intended for corporate entities, like nations, people groups, tribes and sections of the community.

How else can reconciliation take place? And where else does reconciliation need to take place?

John Dawson, in his book *Healing America's Wounds*,[2] helpfully lists the kind of areas that might need to be addressed, under the heading 'Places of Conflict and Broken Relationship'. We have used the same headings but amended the illustrations to suit our own nation.[3] (Repentance and reconciliation is needed in both directions, and between each group or category and God.)

1. Race to race (English to Irish; white British to black West Indian)

2. Class to class (homeowners to the homeless; those in work to those out of work)

3. Culture to culture (British-born to immigrant communities; sub-cultural groups to main culture)

4. Gender to gender (dominant males to discriminated-against females)

5. Vocation to vocation (professional class to working class; employers to employees)

6. Institution to institution (corporate management to organised unions)

7. Region to region (North to South; Yorkshire to Lancashire)

8. Governed to Government (Protesters to public servants; environmentalists to progressives)

9. Religion to religion (Christian to Muslim)

10. Denomination to denomination (Protestant to Catholic; Charismatic to non-Charismatic)

11. Enterprise to enterprise (monopolies and corporate giants to small businesses)

12. Ideology to ideology (Labour to Conservative; fundamentalists to liberals)

13. Nationality to nationality (British to German; British to Jews)

14. Generation to generation (youth to old age; fathers to children)

15. Family to family (neighbour to neighbour; nuclear families to single parent families; marrieds to singles)

And we could add 'Church to people'.[4]

Questions to be Faced

1. How many times does corporate sin have to be confessed?

Until the powerful influence of that sin has been broken. In answer to the question of the disciples, *'How often shall my brother sin against me and I forgive him?'* Jesus said, *'Seventy times seven'* (Matthew 18:22). If that applies to forgiveness it must also apply to confession.

2. Who does the acknowledging of sin?

Those who are convicted and who feel the guilt and shame of it. The acknowledgement of sin can take place at various levels of encounter: between us, the guilty, and God of course; but also between us and the group sinned against; between individuals from the two groups; between the religious leaders of the groups; and between representatives of government.

3. Where should corporate sin be acknowledged?

Anywhere. But there may be specific occasions when it is right to go to the sites where the sin was committed, as for instance the site where a corporate massacre has occurred, and where history constantly remembers the occasion. Wouldn't it be wonderful, for example, if, instead of marching in Northern Ireland in an intimidatory fashion through the areas of past conquest on the anniversaries of battles, Orange Order groups would go and apologise, and ask for forgiveness? And if Black Order groups did the same?

4. What about the sins of other nations or groups towards us?

Although there may be sins to acknowledge, it is not our task to point these out. Those who wish to respond must be free to do so not out of coercion, but out of conviction. This is also true for the injured party. If God wants them to acknowledge their sin, His Holy Spirit can point that out. However, we have never known any public occasion where there has not been acknowledgement of sin on both sides, and this always makes for genuine reconciliation.

Dealing with Corporate Sin and Pain

We will attempt to lay down some guidelines for dealing with corporate sin, healing the pain that is both inflicted and felt by the perpetrators and victims, and breaking the curses which inevitably result. However, we want to avoid developing a specific pattern that is universally applicable. In our experience we have found that God is in charge of the agenda, the timing and the occasion. We have both had experiences where through inadequate preparation, and insufficient biblical teaching, our attempts have not met with the response that is necessary.

On the other hand we have at times been surprised at the way that God has brought something about through an unexpected intervention, or instant and unpremeditated revelation. Sometimes there is someone present in an audience representing a group and a history we know nothing about. If God is working, we have to make room for that exposure, providing it is relevant to the occasion and to the other people present. It is no good, for example, for a Ghanaian to stand up and confess the sins his tribal group has committed against another tribal group or nationality, if nobody from that group is present. His confession is for another time and place.

1. Confront corporate sin biblically

We have sought to give a biblical rationale in chapter 2. As we seek to confront corporate sin there are also other scriptures to help us. In the book of Acts, for example, the apostle Peter is very specific. He confronts the Sanhedrin with the words:

> '... you nailed [Jesus] to a cross by the hands of godless men and put Him to death.'   (Acts 2:23)

They used non-Jews – Roman soldiers – to do the job. In the Crusades nine hundred years ago Church leaders used wicked men to help put Jews, Muslims and other Christian groups to death. So here is a biblical reference point to help us understand how Church leaders have in the past used wicked men to do their dirty work. Peter condemns it, and so must we.

In Acts 3:14–19, Peter again, speaking to the common people, makes some bold points:

- 'You asked for a murderer...'
- 'You put to death the Prince of life...'
- 'I know you acted in ignorance, just as your rulers did also.'

- *'Repent therefore and return . . . '*
- *' . . . that your sins may be wiped away . . . '*
- *' . . . in order that times of refreshing may come from the presence of the Lord.'*

Stephen, in making his defence before the same Sanhedrin, draws their attention to the sins of their forefathers, and what happened as a consequence (Acts 7:39–43). He then accuses them:

- *'Which one of the prophets did your fathers not persecute?'*
- *'You killed those who had previously announced the coming of the Righteous One . . . '*
- *' . . . whose betrayers and murderers you have now become;'*
- *'you who received the law as ordained by angels, and yet did not keep it . . . '*

One of the most telling passages about ancient historical sin is in Matthew 23:29–36, where Jesus highlights the guilt that is centuries old, and its relevance for the generation of the day:

> *'Woe to you, scribes, and Phrarisees, hypocrites! For you build the tombs of the prophets and adorn the monuments of the righteous and say, "If we had been living in the days of our fathers, we would not have been partners with them in shedding the blood of the prophets." '* (Matthew 23:29–30)

But Jesus tells the Pharisees and teachers of the law, prophetically, that they will do the same as their forefathers did, killing the prophets, wise men and teachers:

> *'Some of them you will kill and crucify; and some of them you will scourge in your synagogues, and persecute from city to city, that upon you may fall the guilt of all the righeous blood shed on earth, from the blood of righteous Abel to the blood of Zechariah, the son Berechiah, whom you murdered between the temple and the altar. Truly I say to you, all these things shall come upon this generation.'* (Matthew 23:34–6)

In other words Jesus implies that by doing what their forefathers did, and worse, they will reinforce the guilt of

successive generations – guilt over unconfessed sin. We
believe that failure to repent for past corporate sin allows
the sin to continue so that the shedding of blood from past
generations comes on the present generation. When the
horror of this hits us, we can no longer look accusingly at
others who sin in the tormented trouble spots of the world.
We can only come to God in anguish and shame, repenting
and pleading for forgiveness, and go representationally to
those sinned against to do the same.

2. Confess corporate sin specifically

It is not sufficient to say 'I am guilty', or 'we are guilty', or 'we
are sorry': we need to identify the specific sins that we know
about; and we need to encourage individuals to confess and
repent of the sin on behalf of the group they are part of.

For instance, I may have no personal feelings of animosity
towards people of another race or colour but I may be very
much aware of the way my group (white people) treat them.
So in taking spiritual responsibility, as Daniel did (see Daniel
9), I confess everything that I am aware of and that the Spirit
of God brings to my notice. Not only do I need to name
the sin, but I also need to specify particular expressions
of it known to me – both in its manifestations (superiority,
pride, discrimination, violence and injustice) and particular
occasions when they were expressed, in history and in
contemporary life.

Once this process has been started, God seems to bring out
issues that have never before been faced or perhaps were not
even known about. He takes us deeper and deeper, and
begins to remind us of events and situations where racism
has been demonstrated. What may start off as a one-off
event, may develop as different individuals speak of similar
situations. Meanwhile, our store of knowledge and understanding grows, and the horror of what we are confessing
becomes anguish within our spirits and emotions (as in Ezra
10:1 when Ezra prays, confesses, weeps and throws himself
down before God in anguish and shame).[5]

God may lead us to go to places and peoples among whom
atrocities have been committed, to pray for healing and
forgiveness to flow. Sometimes the memory of massacres is

reinforced in successive generations, as in Ireland. Sometimes spiritual strongholds have been created by the work of Satan feeding on the sin of the Church.

But confession and apology for corporate sin has to be met also with forgiveness from someone representing the group that is offended. They need to say 'I forgive you. We forgive you', and then they need to be encouraged to acknowledge the sins of their group. In the case of racism for example, reserve, mistrust, hatred, criticism and fear may have led to violence in return. So both sides are guilty and need to confess. Neither is guiltless.

3. Confirm the efficacy of Christ's blood

Colossians 2:13–14 reminds us that the cross is the place where forgiveness for our sins has been made possible. This needs to be affirmed publicly, followed by prayer for the covering and the cleansing of Christ's blood-sacrifice to be made effective for all involved. Taking communion together as part of the act of identificational repentance helps to do this very powerfully. In 1 John 1:9 and 2:2 we are reminded of the ground for our forgiveness, and that Christ is the atoning sacrifice for our sin, and also for that of the **whole** world!

4. Confront the spiritual powers and break curses

Having done all that, we then have grounds on which to confront the spiritual powers that have prevailed over the area, or in the group in question through the repeated manifestations of those sins. Paul encourages us to take our stand against the devil's schemes, and against principalities and powers. So we need to do that.

Curses are produced by disobedience and sin among the people of God (Deuteronomy 11:28 and Daniel 9:11). We need also to break the curse that the Church's corporate sin has produced – over both the victims and the perpetrators. If unconfessed sin leads into bondage, then confessed sin leads to freedom from such bondages. We need to break the power of cancelled sin and to pray to turn the curse into a blessing.

5. Celebrate Christ's victory

Finally we celebrate Christ's victory by:

- affirming the positive that is the opposite of the negative (e.g. peace instead of conflict, life instead of death, gladness instead of mourning – see Isaiah 61:3–4);

- lifting up the name of Jesus, and declaring his victory over all sin and the works of Satan;

- encouraging deeds of love, acceptance, and unity between previously segregated groups;

- praying for the Holy Spirit to be poured out, so that where there has previously been barrenness, there will be fruitfulness; where there has been resistance to the gospel, there will be openness;

- praying for God's blessing to flow into and through both parties involved in the confession. It is best if each can do that for the other.

We will also need to pray together that what has happened will spread throughout the Church into other situations, into society and Government where they have been implicated and led astray by the Church's previous bad example.

Notes

1. Darton, Longman & Todd (1995).
2. Published by Regal Books (1994), pp. 117–8.
3. The categories given in brackets are examples, they are not meant to be exclusive.
4. Over issues to do with clearances of land and enclosures see chapter 14.
5. See also Ezra 9:6–7.

Chapter 16

The Tower of London

The Tower of London is Britain's top tourist attraction. This massive castle-cum-fortress on the banks of the River Thames, adjacent to colourful Tower Bridge, has graced thousands of picture postcards sent to all the corners of the earth. In its history, apart from being the Royal Palace, garrison and museum it is today, it has been an armoury, a State prison, a zoo and a place of execution. It is home to 150 Yeoman warders, tower officers and their families, a governor, a detachment of troops from Buckingham Palace, and six ravens and a chaplain! It also houses the Crown jewels.

The Tower's history and reputation make it an obvious tourist attraction. On Christmas Day in 1066, William of Normandy (the Conqueror) was crowned King of England. Ten years later he began transforming what was then a simple fort into the impregnable Tower of London we know today. Over the centuries it has been inextricably linked to royalty, to Government, to trade and commerce, to the armed forces and to the Church.

Like a labyrinth of intertwined strands, the Tower of London has been the site of murders, suicides, betrayals, poisonings, revolts, acts of revenge, and some of the most horrific tortures and cruelty known to humanity. From 1483 to 1941 it was a place of execution of royalty, traitors and common criminals. Beheading was the method most commonly used for noble people, those of lower rank were 'hung, drawn and quartered'. Common criminals were hanged and heretics burned. History reveals the Tower's awful past, linking it to the Reformation, to the Empire, to the East India Company, to the Peasants' Uprising, to Ireland, to the English Civil War, to bishops, buccaneers, explorers, traitors, in fact to almost every significant event of English history over the past nine hundred years. Its fame is coloured by its infamy, its tradition by its superstition, its reputation by its intrigue. Its last recorded prisoner was Rudolf Hess, the Nazi war-criminal, who was held there during the Second World War whilst trying to negotiate a deal with England! Its last execution took place in 1941 when a German spy died at the hands of a firing squad.

In chapter 1 we spoke of the 'spirit of murder', which we believe grips the nation of Britain, and we referred to the Tower connection. Why is it important to highlight a single site in a book dealing with the sins of our nation? Because it symbolises so much in our history that is sinister, and that makes us ashamed and anguished. For half a century the German nation has been going through the pain and agony of its own more recent history. Have we as a nation ever felt the pain of our history? The Tower is, it seems, a symbol of Empire – a bygone era – but nevertheless an era of apparent glory. And yet that glory has been tarnished by sins committed both at home and abroad.

The truth is that many of the Empire roads lead back to the Tower. Leading members of the Church have been tried and executed there. Monarchs and individuals connected to the royal family have been beheaded there. Like a giant octopus with tentacles reaching out in all directions, its head has been the source of its strength, and the place to which its victims and enemies have been brought in final, terrifying submission.

There is some evidence that Tower Hill in London was a place of significance even in ancient Britain. In ancient mythology Bran, the god-king, who according to Celtic custom was guardian of the city, requested that his head be brought back to the tower on the hill in London, when he realised he was mortally wounded in a battle with the Irish! The ravens are said to be his birds watching over London for him. Even then it may have been a place of human sacrifice to appease the gods and the water spirits.

It was also an important shipping port. Merchants from London loaded and unloaded their ships there and, like the ports of Bristol and Liverpool, it was linked to the slave trade.

In his account of the building of the Tower of London, William Fitzsteplhen, a twelfth-century chronicler, states that the mortar was mixed with the blood of beasts. That may refer to a custom in which blood from the sacrifice of animals was used as a substitute for human sacrifice.

Some of the blood shed at the Tower in later centuries was innocent. The Archbishop of Canterbury was executed there in 1381; Sir Thomas More and Bishop John Fisher were imprisoned and then murdered there. Their crime? Refusing to take the Oath of Supremacy following Henry VIII's secession from the influence of the Roman Church. In 1581 Edmund Campion, who had been arrested for his book attacking the Anglican Church, was tried and sentenced to be hanged, drawn and quartered. Conspirators, adulterers, nine MPs, 267 Jews, two young princes, unfaithful wives and courtiers have all died there. Jacobites were imprisoned and later executed. Many Scots suffered the same fate after the Battle of Culloden in 1745. Most of this blood was shed at the time when the Tower was the seat of Government.

The Peasants' Revolt in 1381, protesting against the way the Church and landowners had robbed so many peasants of their land forcing them into poverty, centred on the Tower. The rebels ransacked the Tower, and while the royal family escaped, four of the King's ministers were beheaded on Tower Hill.

In the Middle Ages public executions were watched by unruly crowds numbering many thousands. Special stands had to be created to accommodate them all. On one occasion a stand collapsed killing many people. The Dark Ages were supposed to have ended before the Reformation in 1536, but this must have been one of the most murderous periods in our history.

It was during Henry VIII's reign and the Reformation that followed, that the Tower experienced its most bloody era. Yet throughout this time and before, the Tower was the place from which coronation processions began. The split between the Crown and Parliament and the ensuing Civil War centred on the Tower too. The Commander of the King's last army, which was fortified in the Tower, surrendered giving Parliament control over the Tower and London.

When sin is repeatedly committed by individuals, there comes a time when God gives them over to the due reward of their sins. Without repentance there is only judgement to be faced. The same must surely be true of corporate groups or nations. In Romans 1, the Apostle Paul uses the plural when he writes:

> *'And just as they did not see fit to acknowledge God any longer, God gave them over to a depraved mind, to do those things which are not proper, being filled with all unrighteousness, wickedness, **greed**, evil; full of envy, **murder**, strife, deceit, malice; they are gossips, slanderers, haters of God, insolent, arrogant, boastful, inventors of evil, disobedient to parents, without understanding, untrustworthy, unloving, unmerciful; and, although they know the ordinance of God, that those who practice such things are worthy of death, they not only do the same, but also give hearty approval to those who practice them.'*
>
> (Romans 1:28–32, emphasis mine)

Here God is not only judging the guilty, but also those who sanction them or acquiesce in their depraved deeds. Surely the finger of God is pointing at us as a nation, and as a Church in this nation. Although there have been times when the Church has been persecuted and its leaders executed, there have also been times when it has not acted in grace and humility. We have too easily indulged in the same kinds of sins as the nation, or supported those who have been serving King, country, and Church with unrighteous means.

When the Church (our forefathers acting in God's name either righteously or unrighteously) commits sin it is wrong. When they (or we) persist in the same kind of sin, we allow Satan to build a stronghold of evil. We create a climate that in effect says, 'we've done this or sanctioned that. It's OK – you can do it as well.' What is our root sin? As we have already suggested, we believe it is greed – the love of money – which is the root of all evil.

> *'What is the source of quarrels and conflicts among you? Is*
> *not the source your pleasures that wage war in your members?*
> *You lust and do not have; so you commit murder. And you are*
> *envious and cannot obtain; so you fight and quarrel. You do*
> *not have because you do not ask.'* (James 4:1–2)

And there you have it!

Can places become demonic strongholds? We believe the answer is 'yes'. Jacob, after he wrestled with the angel of God, commented:

> *'Surely the Lord is in this place, and I did not know it ... How*
> *awesome is this place! This is none other than the house of*
> *God and this is the gate of heaven.'* (Genesis 28:16–17)

God was in the place – Jacob sensed it, although not at the time, but later. In Revelation 2 the church at Pergamum was in the place *'where Satan's throne is; and you hold fast My name, and did not deny My faith, even in the days of Antipas, My witness, My faithful one, who was killed among you, where Satan dwells'* (Revelation 2:13). It was a place of immorality and extreme idolatry. Pergamum was the chief town of the new province of Asia, and the site of the first temple of the Caesar-cult. A second shrine was dedicated later to Trajan. The worship of Asklepios and Zeus was also endemic. The symbol of the former was a serpent, and Pausanias describes his cult image 'with a staff in one hand and the other on the head of the serpent'. On the crag above Pergamum was a huge throne-like altar to Zeus, now located in the Pergamum museum in Berlin. 'Zeus, to deepen Christian horror at Pergamum's obsession with the serpent-image, was called "Zeus the Saviour".'[1]

The point we wish to make is that here was a place where it was extremely difficult to survive as a Christian – a place where Satan lived – and yet the Church remained true to Christ's name. Would that the Church had been more faithful throughout the period and places covered in this book! If Pergamum was a physical place where so much evidence of Satan's activity was present, might not London and its Tower be a similar place? And if that is so, what can we do about it? And does that mean that there is no good there at all? No, it doesn't. There was righteousness in the midst of the evil at Pergamum, and today there is a witness for Christ in the chapel within the Tower. Daily prayer still goes on there.

Can the people living in a city or nation become influenced by that demonic presence and affected by the prevailing sin, almost against their will? Again we believe the answer is 'yes'. We live in a materialistic society. As Christians we become affected and influenced by that, so that we too become materialistic. We have to make a conscious choice to go against the grain. Even when we do, we only have to go into other cultures to realise how materialistic we still remain. People living in Ireland or the Balkans or Rwanda also become affected by the religious, ethnic or tribal hatreds. They are brought up in the atmosphere of blame, fear and recrimination. It is only when they move out of their country that they begin to realise how affected and controlled they have been. People inevitably become affected by the prevailing sin, and the demonic presence behind that sin.

Nineveh was described as 'a very wicked city'. God pronounced judgement on it and its inhabitants. But he also showed His mercy by sending Jonah to call it to repentance. Even though Jonah disobeyed, God still wished to show His mercy. Nineveh was not part of God's eternal purposes. It had been built by Nimrod, the mighty hunter, and was the capital of the Assyrian empire. When the message was delivered, the king took the lead in repenting, and pleaded with the nation to *'call on God earnestly that each may turn from his wicked way and from the violence which is in his hands'* (Jonah 3:8). There are many more examples of corporate repentance on behalf of cities, tribes and nations. Each time God was merciful, judgement was stayed, and a period of renewal occurred.

But is there more that we can do? We believe so. When we confess our own corporate sin – today's and yesterday's – and seek forgiveness firstly from God and secondly from those we have so harmed, we will turn away reproach from our nation. Satan will have his source of power withdrawn. Maternus, a fourth-century Roman Christian, said, 'demons are particularly attracted to the blood of sacrificed victims'. One can understand why and how that may be so. If we take away the source of Satan's power we begin to starve him of his authority and he has to retreat. As the Body of Christ we can then issue him with an eviction notice and at the same time renew our covenant of love with God, with one another and with those we have offended. Then we will have begun to lay a foundation of righteousness on which God can build once more.

The British Empire is no more. We have given the lands we once owned back to their indigenous populations. We have granted nations their independence. Sometimes we have done so grudgingly, and sometimes not without bloodshed; sometimes we have entered quickly into treaties so as to extricate ourselves from situations we could no longer adequately control. It may have seemed prudent at the time but it may also have been interpreted as running away from the problems we helped to create.

Our Royal Family has been in some disarray. In the 1990s it suffered the ignominy of three messy divorces, including that of the Prince of Wales, the future king. It has been frequently villified by the media and its method of working and its public image questioned. The horrific death of Diana, Princess of Wales, in a car accident brought about unprecedented scenes of national mourning. During the now famous *'annus horribilis'*, 1992, one of its palaces, Windsor Castle, was seriously damaged by fire. One is left asking how much of this is due in part to our corporate history? Have we as Christians prayed sufficiently for the Royal Family (see 1 Timothy 2:1–3)? Have we begun to deal adequately with the demonic powers that have fed on the shedding of innocent blood through the centuries? Have we realised that empires built on injustice, crime and bloodshed inevitably fall and fail? These are the questions we need to face.

On the credit side, there have been occasions when leading members of Church and State have apologised to nations that we have offended in our history. Such acts may need to be repeated many, many more times. Hosea 6:8–10 tells us that:

> *'Gilead is a city of wrongdoers, tracked with bloody footprints.*
> *And as raiders wait for a man, so a band of priests murder on*
> *the way to Shechem; surely they have committed crime.'*

Priests involved in murder? Can children of God do the same? Unfortunately, yes. Priests corrupted by greed? Can children of God be the same? Unfortunately, yes.

We can't undo our history. It is there to haunt us. But what we can do is to face it – the bad parts as well as the good. For too long we have only looked at the good and have failed to acknowledge the bad. Maybe God will begin to be gracious to us and to those we have hurt when we begin to acknowledge before God and those we have so offended our shame and sin, seeking their forgiveness. We may also need in appropriate ways to engage in forms of restitution.

We don't understand all the historical connections. We are not investigative journalists. We realise we may occasionally have drawn conclusions that are questionable. What we have sought to do is to reflect on what God has been revealing to us in all kinds of ways. We have been gazing at ourselves and our sin, past and present. We have done so in order that we as God's people can face it, turn from it and be reconciled – to God and others. The alternative is to be a nation that will continue to deserve judgement. We haven't looked at all our corporate sins, only those which God has made us aware of. There are many other nations which feel offended by us – too many to deal with in a book such as this.

Why has this book been written? Our hearts' desire is for us as a nation to become a blessing to the nations in spiritual, cultural and economic ways. If we have exported a gospel defiled by our history, then let us now go in a humble spirit and with love, instead of that which used to characterise our going. If we have robbed peoples of their culture and sought to impose our own, let us now allow them to rediscover their culture. Let us then be enriched by theirs, and share with them some of our own creativity. If we have taken their wealth and resources to make ourselves rich, let us be prepared to be generous, empowering them with our wealth in order to help lift them out of their poverty. Instead of bringing death and destruction, we want to come in the opposite spirit – bringing life and creativity. Is that a vain hope? Isn't that what the Church should be doing anyway?

The finger of God in the Bible is not only associated with judgement. Pharaoh recognised God's finger in the judgements that came on Egypt although his change of mind was usually short-lived (see Exodus 8:19). Belshazzar saw the finger of God write on the wall at his feast (Daniel 5:5). It was God's finger which wrote the Ten Commandments – and how many of them have we as a nation broken? But Christ's ministry of deliverance from demons was also undertaken with the finger of God (see Luke 11:20).

That is our hope. God points at sin in order to be merciful, to deliver us from the demons that feed on that sin, and to bring in the kingdom of God.

Lord, Your kingdom come, Your will be done on earth as it is in heaven ... For Yours is the kingdom, and the power, and the glory, forever and ever. Amen.

Note

1. *Zondervan Pictorial Bible Dictionary*, edited by Merrill C. Tenney (Zondervan Publishing Co., 1988), p. 636.

If you have enjoyed this book and would like to help us to
send a copy of it and many other titles to needy pastors in
the **Third World,** please write for further information
or send your gift to:

Sovereign World Trust
PO Box 777, Tonbridge
Kent TN11 0ZS
United Kingdom

or to the **'Sovereign World'** distributor in your country.